THE SECRET OF
THE RUNES

BY

Guido von List

EDITED, INTRODUCED, AND TRANSLATED

BY

Stephen E. Flowers

Destiny Books
Rochester, Vermont

Inner Traditions International, Ltd.
One Park Street
Rochester, Vermont 05767

Library of Congress Cataloging-in-Publication Data
List, Guido, 1848–1919.
The secret of the Runes.
Translation of: Das Geheimnis der Runen.
Bibliography: p.
Includes index.
1. Runes—Miscellanea. 2. Occultism.
3. List, Guido, 1848–1919. I. Flowers,
Stephen E., 1953–   . II. Title.
BF1623.R89L5713 1988   133.3'3   88-768
ISBN 0-89281-207-9 (pbk.)

10 9 8 7 6 5 4 3 2 1

Printed and bound in the United States.

Distributed to the book trade in the United States
by Harper and Row Publishers, Inc.
Distributed to the book trade in Canada by Book Center, Inc.,
Montreal, Quebec

THE SECRET OF
THE RUNES

Table of The Secret of the Runes by Guido von List

ᚠ ᚢ ᚦ ᛆ ᚱ ᚴ ᚼ ᚾ ᛁ ᛆ ᛋ ᛏ ᛒ ᛚ ᛘ ᛦ ᛂ

fa·ur·thurs·os·rit·ka·hag·not·is·ar·sol·tyr·bar·laf·man·yr·eh· two bound together by law ge, gi

F U Th A·O·R·K H N I A S T B L M Y E · · G

Trifos Vilfos Fylfos Turn-foot Three-foot Fyrfos Hook-cross Four-foot Ruoth-cross Fire-whisk Head of Gereon [Trimsfi]

per pale, sinister a bar sinister | upper pale rompu | lower pale rompu | dexter fess fracted bevelled | sinister fess fracted square | downward fracted bar sinister

dexter bend fracted | per bend with counter pile | with counter pile bend | with counter wedge bend | quarterly per square | quarterly per wavy

Fyrfos, or Hook Cross | Cross Gringol | T-Square Cross | Cross Potent | Jerusalem Cross | Arrow Cross

Cross Botonée | Cross Fleury | Cross Moline | Concealed Fyrfos | Maltese Cross | Cross of Pyrmont

Trifoil | Flamboyant Trifoil | Quadrafoil | Flamboyant Quadrafoil

Vehme-Star Rose [Pentagram] | Saint Catherine's Wheel [Ruoth Cross] | Vehme Cross | Fyroge, Tapis, Tabula quadrata with the three great lights

Plate of runic symbols with original illustrations by Guido von List. From *Das Geheimnis der Runen*, first published in Vienna, Austria, 1908.

ACKNOWLEDGMENTS

I would like to thank Professor Edgar C. Polomé for reading the manuscript of this work and for making helpful suggestions on its improvement. This was but one small example of the guidance he has provided me over the years. Also I would like to acknowledge the influence of Dr. Robert Mollenauer in directing my attention to the literary aspects of the works of List and others.

CONTENTS

PREFACE

THE time has come to let Guido von List at last speak for himself to the English reading public. With the possible exception of Lanz von Liebenfels, no other figure of the German "occult" movements of the late nineteenth and early twentieth centuries has been more misrepresented than List. This work will, it is hoped, help to set the record straight on the exact nature and scope of "Armanism" and the pre–National Socialist neo-Germanic cult of the early part of this century.

The original impetus for this book came in 1973 when I first picked up a copy of Trevor Ravenscroft's work *The Spear of Destiny*.[1] I found the contents of that book utterly fascinating and intriguing. But it must be added that I was only twenty years old at the time. What the book did, however, was fuel my interest in the study of Germanic and neo-Germanic mysticism. It seemed to be unique from that most readily available for study, that is, the systems based on Mediterranean, Middle Eastern, and Eastern ideas.

After studying the content of the book, much of which seemed to give specific leads for further research, I began to acquire the works of List, Liebenfels, and others. As my collection and knowledge of the works and ideas of these men grew, it became quite obvious that they had been—at least factually—mis-represented by Ravenscroft.

In any case, it seems appropriate that an ideologue who, according to different sources, was such a great influence on the events of this century should at least have a study dedicated solely to his life and ideas. To this end, I have introduced List's first systematic occult treatise—*Das Geheimnis der Runen*—with a general outline of his life and works.

STEPHEN E. FLOWERS
Austin, March 1987

INTRODUCTION

ALTHOUGH *The Secret of the Runes* was originally
intended as an introduction to List's basic ideas, and
contains examples of virtually all of his major themes,
a general overview of the life, work, and reception of
this remarkable man are necessary to a more thorough
understanding of his ultimate historical importance.
The purpose of this introduction is to present List's
ideas as clearly and completely as possible, and with
a minimum of the sensationalism or subtle condem-
nations in which treatments of him are usually
couched. It is assumed that the intelligent reader will
be able to decide for himself whether there is any
mystical validity to List's work. In some instances
factual errors or linguistic fallacies in List's text have
been noted.

Besides the particulars of List's life, literary works,
and ideology, it is essential to explore the possible
origins of his concepts and the reception of those ideas
during and after his own lifetime. It is rather aston-
ishing that so little is actually known about this man
who was virtually a "legend in his own time." The
reasons for this seem clear enough, however. Like
most cult leaders—and true magicians—List had a
vested interest in controlling and manipulating information concerning his person. After his death, his
followers continued to have similar motives. Only

one book-length biography of List exists, that of the Theosophist and Armanist Johannes Balzli (1917).[2] Balzli's book was actually issued as an introduction to List's published series of "investigative findings" (*Forschungsergebnisse*), and so it can hardly be considered objective. By far the most reliable treatment of at least some of List's ideas is that of Nicholas Goodrick-Clarke.[3] But the limitations placed upon this study by the thesis of his original dissertation—that is, "reactionary political fantasy in relation to social anxiety"—renders a less-than-well-rounded picture.

THE LIFE OF GUIDO VON LIST

Early Life (1848–1869)

GUIDO KARL ANTON LIST was born in Vienna on 5 October 1848 to Karl August and Maria List (née Killian). His father was a fairly prosperous dealer in leather goods, and we can assume that Guido's early life was lived in comfortable and nurturing surroundings. The List family was Catholic, and we also presume that Guido was trained in that confession.

From the time of adolescence we have evidence of some of his propensities in life. He was fascinated by the landscape of his native Lower Austria and by the cityscape of his native city, Vienna. His sketchbook—which has drawings from as far back as 1863 (when he would have been fifteen years old)—demonstrates his interest in such sites. Some of these sketches were later used to illustrate the *Deutsch-mythologische Landschaftsbilder* (German Mythological Landscape Scenes, published 1891).[4] In conjunction with the romanticizing of his environment, young Guido, by his own account,[5] also had developed a strong mystomagical bent of no orthodox variety.

It was in the year 1862—I was then in my fourteenth year of life—when I, after much asking, received permission from my father to accompany him and his party who were planning to visit the catacombs [under St. Stephen's Cathedral in Vienna] which were at that time still in their original condition. We climbed down, and everything I saw and felt excited me with a kind of power that today I am no longer able to experience. Then we came—it was, if I remember correctly, in the third or fourth level—to a ruined altar. The guide said that we were now situated beneath the old post office (today the Wohlzeile House No. 8). At that point my excitement was raised to fever pitch, and before this altar I proclaimed out loud this ceremonial vow: "Whenever I get big, I will build a Temple of Wotan!" I was, of course, laughed at, as a few members of the party said that a child did not belong in such a place. . . . I knew nothing more about Wuotan than that which I had read about him in Vollmer's *Wörterbuch der Mythologie*.[6]

Despite these artistic and mystical leanings, Guido was expected, as the eldest child, to follow in his father's footsteps as a businessman. He appears to have fulfilled his responsibilities in a dutiful manner, but he took any and all opportunities to develop his more intense interests.

The Mystic Wanderer (1870–77)

The many trips that List was obliged to make for business purposes afforded him the opportunity to indulge himself in his passion for hiking and mountaineering. This activity seems to have provided a matrix for his early mysticism.

Although descriptions of List's early pilgrimages into nature exist,[7] it is unclear what underlying mystical tradition he was familiar with at that time. Two things are obvious, however: he was possessed of the idea of the sacrality of his *native land*, and he had an unwaivering belief in the sacrality of *nature*, or the "All-Mother." The interest in his native soil was prob-

ably spurred by his early passion for Germanic myth
and lore.[8]

At one point, one of his mountain adventures almost claimed List's life. As he was climbing a mountain on 8 May 1871, a mass of ice gave way under his
feet and he fell some distance. He was apparently
saved only by the fact that he had landed on a soft
surface covered by a recent snowfall. In memory of
his good luck List had a track equipped with a chain
put up. This was opened on 21 June 1871 and was
named after him: the Guido-List-Steig.[9]

Apparently List recorded his mystical wanderings
in nature in verbal descriptions as well as in sketches.
In 1871, his writing talents were given vent as he
became a correspondent of the *Neue deutsche Alpenzeitung* (New German Alpine Newspaper), later
called the *Salonblatt*. He also began to edit the year-
book of the *Österreicher Alpenverein* (Austrian Alpine Association), whose secretary he had become that
year.

List often went in the company of others on his
journeys into the mountains, which were taken on
foot, by wagon, horse, or rowboat; but he would usually strike out on his own at some point to seek the
solitude of nature.

Besides gaining general mystical impressions in these
outings, List also engaged in active celebratory ritual
work. He would perform various rituals that sometimes seemed quite impromptu. The most famous
depiction of such an event is his celebration of the
summer solstice on 24 June 1875 at the ruins of the
Roman City of Carnuntum.[10] For this—as for so much
else—we are dependent on List's own somewhat fictionalized account, first published in Vienna in 1881.

Basically, the ritual elements of this outing included the arduous task of gaining access to the so-
called *Heidentor* ("Heathen Gate") of the city (which
List mystically identified as the gate from which a

German army set out to conquer Rome in 375 C.E.), the drinking of ritual toasts to the memory of the local spirit *(genius loci)* and the heroes of the past, the lighting of a solstice fire, and the laying of eight wine bottles in the shape of the "fyrfos" (swastika) in the glowing embers of the fire. List and his company then awaited the dawn.

These early experiences were sometimes later more completely fictionalized, as, for example, in his visionary tale "Eine Zaubernacht" (A Night of Magic).[11] In this account, the persona (List) succeeds in invoking from the great mound a divine seeress *(Hechsa)* who reveals to him that he is not to be the liberator of the Germans—but that despite this "the German folk has need of the skald."

The Folkish Journalist (1877–87)

This rather comfortable, if self-divided, period in List's life came to an end after his father died in 1877, when List was twenty-nine years old. Neither he nor his mother appear to have had the elder List's keen sense of business, and as economic times became difficult List quit the business to devote himself fulltime to his writing. At this time his writing continued to be of a journalistic kind. Deprived of his ability to travel and wander as he had before, he wrote articles for newspapers, such as the *Neue Welt, Neue deutsche Alpenzeitung, Heimat,* and the *Deutsche Zeitung,* which dealt with his earlier travels and mystical reflections on these *loci.* Many of these pieces were anthologized in 1891 in his famous *Deutsch-mythologische Landschaftsbilder.* It was also during this period, in 1878, that he married his first wife, Helene Föster-Peters. However, the marriage was not to last through the difficult years of this period.

Given the Pan-German nationalism of the various groups and papers with which List had been associated throughout his career, it seems certain that from a political standpoint he was firmly in their camp.[12] However, the nature of his mysticism at this time seems to have been somewhat more original. Before any influence from later Theosophical notions could have been present, he was continuing on the path of mystical Germanic revivalism. Besides his own intuition—which, given his results, must have been his chief source—he must have been familiar with a variety of nonscientific, neoromantic works on Germanic mythology and religion popular at the time,[13] and was perhaps also aware of at least a portion of the scientific studies. In any event, many of the uniquely Listian notions seem to have been already solidifying in this early period.

Through these years, List was also working on his first book-length (two-volume) effort, *Carnuntum*, a historical novel based on his vision of the *Kulturkampf* between the Germanic and Roman worlds centered at that location around the year 375 C.E.

The Nationalist Poet (1888–98)

Carnuntum was published in 1888 and became a huge success, especially among the Pan-German nationalists of Austria and Germany. Its publication brought its author more to the attention of important political and economic leaders of German nationalist movements. In connection with the appearance of *Carnuntum*, List made the acquaintance of the industrialist Friedrich Wannieck. This association was to prove essential to List's future development.

Throughout this period, List devoted himself to the production of further neoromantic prose, such as *Jung Diethers Heimkehr* (Young Diether's Homecoming) and *Pipara*, in 1894 and 1895 respectively. The anthology of earlier journalism *Deutsch-mythologische Landschaftsbilder* was published in 1891, and List developed his writing skills in poetic and dramatic genres as well.

List became involved with two important literary associations during these years. In May 1891, the Iduna, bearing the descriptive subtitle "Free German Society for Literature," was founded by a circle of writers around Fritz Lemmermayer. Lemmermayer acted as a sort of "middle man" between an older generation of authors (which included Fercher von Steinwand, Joseph Tandler, Auguste Hyrtl, Ludwig von Mertens, and Josephine von Knorr) and a group of younger writers and thinkers (which included Rudolf Steiner, Marie Eugenie delle Grazie, and Karl Maria Heidt). The name *Iduna*, which was provided by List himself, is that of a North Germanic goddess of eternal youth and renewal. Within the society were two other authors with specifically neo-Germanic leanings: Richard von Kralik and Joseph Kalasanz Poestion. This literary circle was loosely held together by neoromantic ideas of German nationalism, a sense of "turning within one's self" *(innerliche Wanderung)*, antirealism, and anti-decadence. The society was only able to last until 1893, when the dilettantism of the various interests seems to have become too acute. However, in many ways this does seem to have been the springtime of the neo-Germanic movement.[14] Another neoromantic literary association, the Literarische Donaugesell-schaft (Danubian Literary Society), was founded by List and Fanny Wschiansky the year the Iduna was dissolved.[15]

It is almost certain that List and Rudolf Steiner knew each other in the early 1890s, since both were members of the Iduna. It is also certain that both were being influenced by the first waves of Theosophy and occult revivalism in German-speaking countries at that time. However, there is little chance that either one had too much direct influence on the other. Each of them would become more "Theosophical" in the next decade. List also met the young Jörg Lanz von Liebenfels (Adolf Joseph) at this time as well—but it would not be until after Lanz had left the Heiligen-kreuz monastery in 1899 that any extensive interaction between the two was possible.

By far the most important influences on List's development at this time were those provided by the nationalist and Pan-German cultural and political groups whose attention had been drawn to him by the publication of *Carnuntum*. These were largely associations of people of German ancestry and language in the multiethnic Austrian Empire, whose aims included the promotion of Germanic culture and language (over that of non-German subjects) and the eventual political union of Austrian Germans with the greater German Empire to the west, that is, Germany proper.[16]

Of course such notions were common enough at the time, and List was certainly already firmly in this camp before 1891. Even the "sporting" associations in which he had earlier begun to be active had Pan-German political aims. However, this period began a more activist phase for List, who had, up until this time, been fairly exclusively "mystical" in his approach. The new phase brought List into close contact with such leading political figures as Georg von Schönerer, an anti-Semitic Pan-German member of the Imperial Parliament,[17] and the powerful publicist and parliamentary deputy Karl Wolf. Both of these men also published newspapers, and List's work appeared in Wolf's *Ostdeutsche Rundschau* (East German Review) on a regular basis.[18] It might also be speculated that List had as much a "mystifying" effect on the political world as it had a politicizing effect on his views. This trend would continue with the later advent of the New Templar Jörg Lanz von Liebenfels.

But it was List's association with the Wannieck family and their organization and publishing house,

Verein "Deutsches Haus" ("German House" Association), which was to prove most important to List.
They published many of his books in this decade and
gave him a wider outlet for his ideas. In 1892 he delivered a lecture on the ancient Germanic cult of
Wuotan to the Verein Deutsche Geschichte (German
History Association). Numerous other associations
allied with this one proliferated in Austria at this
time. Another group, the Bund der Germanen (Germanic League), sponsored the performance of List's
mythological dramatic poem, *Der Wala Erweckung*
(The Wala's Awakening), in 1894. In another performance of this drama in 1895, which was attended by
over three thousand people, the part of the Wala was
read by Anna Wittek, a young actress who later became List's second wife.

Through these years, List became a well-known and
respected artist and mystagogue among Austrian German nationalists, and he was to remain a part of the
conservative cultural establishment throughout his
life.

The Emerging Master (1898–1902)

The time between the publication of *Der Unbesiegbare* (1898), List's neo-Germanic catechism, and the
year 1902 marked a period of transformation of List
from someone known primarily as an artist to an occult investigator, religious leader, and prophet of a
coming age.

Concerning the generation of the manuscript for
Der Unbesiegbare there is a story that perhaps demonstrates the growing—if ambivalent—association
between mysticism and politics in these circles. In
the summer of 1898, a law prescribing religious in-
struction in Lower Austrian secondary schools was
being debated. Dr. Karl Lueger, who was later to become the mayor of Vienna and a member of the Guido

von List Society, was for the bill, as were church of-
ficials. When he was questioned on this by representative Karl Wolf, Lueger responded: "Gebt uns
Besseres und wir werden Euch folgen!" (Give us something better and we shall follow you!). It is said that
List was deeply moved by this and wrote *Der Unbesiegbare* overnight. List took the manuscript to
Wolf's office the next day, but the whole idea was
eventually rejected by Wolf, as his interests in religion
were "just matters of curriculum." The catechism
was printed in an edition of five thousand copies,[19]
marking the beginning of List's more practical religious career.

Perhaps the successes he had had with the poetic
drama *Der Wala Erweckung* spurred List to try his
hand at more drama, because in the last phase of his
conventional literary career this genre predominated.
However, to assume that List intended these dramas
as mere entertainment would be a mistake. He saw
them more as *Weihespiele* (sacral plays) which had a
liturgical as well as didactic purpose. In 1900, he published a pamphlet, *Der Wiederaufbau von Carnuntum* (The Reconstruction of Carnuntum), in which
he called for the establishment of ritual dramas and
legal assemblies based on ancient Germanic models.

In August 1899, List married Anna Wittek von
Stecky, who had sung the Wala part in his play in
1895. They were married in a Lutheran church—which
is also some indication of the decay of the Catholic
establishment and general religious dissatisfaction in
Austria at that time.

This period acts as a sort of bridge between List's
long artistic phase and his shorter, but highly intense
and influential, mystico-magical phase from 1902 to
his death in 1919. It is also most likely that during
this period (1898–1902) Theosophical ideas as such
became more influential in List's worldview. After
all, it was not until 1897–1901 that the German trans-

lation of *The Secret Doctrine* by H. P. Blavatsky appeared. Certainly List would have had Theosophical ideas available to him long before this (perhaps as early as the 1880s), but the evidence of a general lack of Theosophical concepts in *Der Unbesiegbare* would indicate that it was of little influence before 1898.

In 1902, by his own accounts, there occurred an event that transformed List's life and resulted in his "revelations" concerning the "secret of the runes."

The Occult Master (1902–1919)

Late in 1902, List had undergone an operation for cataracts (see p. 41 below). For eleven months his eyes were bandaged, and in this virtual state of blindness and utter darkness List is said to have been enlightened with regard to the "secret of the runes." At this time, and by whatever means, List's occult vision did seem to undergo a major synthesis. That the main features of his thought were solidified in this period is witnessed by the fact that he produced his first manuscript on *kala* and published an article on his interpretation of glyphs (the swastika, triskelion, etc.) in 1903.[20]

Between this time and 1908, when *Das Geheimnis der Runen* was published and the Guido-von-List-Gesellschaft (Guido von List Society) was founded, List's ideas probably underwent their final synthesis. After 1908, it seems that "occult wisdom" flowed freely and constantly from the pen of the Master.

It was between 1903 and 1907 that List first began to use the noble title "von" in his name.[21] Legitimate or not, it was important for List to distance himself from his middle-class background as his ideas took on a more aristocratic tone—and began to appeal more and more to the aristocratic establishment.

On 2 March 1908 the Guido von List Society was officially founded to support the work of the Master.

Although chiefly founded by the Wannieck family, it was also supported by many leading figures in Austrian and German politics, publishing, and occultism.

All of List's occult research works that were to be published in his lifetime were originally published between 1908 and 1914. Economic restrictions after that time put an end to the production of original works.

The Guido von List Society remained the exoteric outlet for List's ideas, mainly in the form of his multivolume "research findings." However, his work implied a deeper, more practical level as well. For the expression of this aspect, in the form of a magical order or lodge, the Hoher Armanen-Orden (High Armanic Order), HAO, was founded in midsummer 1911. Thus List had formed exoteric and esoteric circles in his organization. The activities of the esoteric HAO were indeed mysterious. We know that they conducted pilgrimages to holy Armanic sites, Saint Stephen's Cathedral in Vienna, Carnuntum, etc. They also had other occasional meetings between 1911 and 1918, but the exact nature of these remains unknown. The HAO never really crystallized in List's lifetime— although it seems possible that he developed a theoretical body of unpublished documents and rituals relevant to the HAO which have only been put into full practice in more recent years.[22]

An odd chapter in Guido von List's story was opened in November 1911 when he received a letter from a mysterious figure in Germany calling himself Tarnhari.[23] This man turned out to be one Ernst Lautner, who claimed to be a descendant of the ancient Nordic tribe of the Wölsungen (Old Norse *Völsungar*, the tribe to which Sigurd/Siegfried belonged). He also claimed, however, to be a reincarnation of a chieftain of this tribe.[24] Lautner was also to be instrumental in the spread of List's ideas in Germany.

Throughout the years of World War I, although

nothing new was published by the Master, his reputation and fame grew, and his ideas were becoming more popular than ever. But the war took its toll on the health of the now elderly List. Within a few months after the end of the war, List died while on a visit to his followers in Berlin, on 17 May 1919.[25] His body was cremated and placed in an urn in his native Vienna.

THE WORKS OF GUIDO VON LIST

The Early Period

BEFORE his mystical "initiation" in 1902 and the
subsequent publication of *Das Geheimnis der Runen*,
Guido von List had, with the notable exception of *Der
Unbesiegbare*, mainly confined himself to journalistic and fiction work. His journalism, however, covered a wide range of material. Much of it was concerned
with the local antiquities and natural and man-made
wonders of the Austrian countryside. But there was
also the occasional foray into actual religious or magical ideas, as in "Götterdämmerung" (1893),[26] "Von
der Wuotanspriesterschaft" (1893),[27] "Die deutsche
Mythologie im Rahmen eines Kalenderjahres" (1894),[28]
"Der deutsche Zauberglaube im Bauwesen" (1895),[29]
and "Mephistopheles" (1895).[30] These, as well as the
natural-mystical assumptions that underlie his interpretations of ancient and natural phenomena, would
seem to indicate that a fairly sophisticated system
of mystical thinking had been developed by List
throughout these early years.

Of course, the major part of List's energies before
1902 were spent in the production of neoromantic
fiction and verse. In this period, basically that between 1888 and 1903, when the last of his major fiction was published, there are essentially two phases.

The first of these, between 1888 and 1895, might be called his novelistic phase. During this time he produced three major novels (including his earlier work *Carnuntum*) and two major epic-dramatic poems.

Carnuntum, his first novel, was set in the time of the Germanic invasions across the Roman *limes* in the late fourth century C.E. Historically, Carnuntum was overrun in 374 C.E. by the Quadi, a Germanic tribe. It is an explicit feature of List's historical vision that modern Austria south and west of the Danube was an *Urheimat*, a primeval homeland, of the Germanic peoples, and that with such ancient invasions the Germans were merely reclaiming territories lost to Roman forces of occupation.[31]

Jung Diethers Heimkehr (1894) is set in the same geographical area in the fifth century. It relates the story of a young Markomanni-Quadi warrior who is forced to convert to Christianity (in the hated Roman culture) but who eventually returns to the faith of his fathers—Wuotanism—once he realizes the essence of "Christianism." In the same year, *Der Wala Erweckung* appeared, but apparently it was not performed until 3 November 1895. In 1895 there also appeared the skaldic sacral drama *Walkürenweihe*. The year 1895 also saw List's most successful work of fiction, *Pipara: Die Germanin im Cäsarenpurpur* (Pipara: the Germanic Woman in the Purple of the Caesars). This two-volume work recounts the legendary rise of a Germanic slave to the position of empress in the late third century C.E.

Probably as a result of his marriage in 1899 to the actress Anna Witteck, List devoted his literary efforts almost exclusively to drama between that year and the year of his final fiction publications, 1903. These included *König Vannius* (1899), *Sommer-Sonnwend-Feuerzauber* (1901), and *Das Goldstück* (1903).

The year 1903 also saw the publication of List's

Kunstmärchen anthology: *Alraunenmären: Kultur-historische Novellen und Dichtungen aus germanischer Vorzeit* (Mandrake-Tales: Cultural-historical Novellas and Poetry from Germanic Prehistory). In this volume List presented original tales and poetry chronologically arranged from the "age of the gods" to the present (in the symbolically autobiographical *"Eine Zaubernacht,"* which recounts his inner experience on that famous visit to Carnuntum in the summer of 1875).

The Later Period

The spiritual watershed year was, of course, 1902. But it was not until 1908 that the first volume of his eight books of "investigations" appeared. Six of these were published by the Guido von List Society itself in the series called the Guido-von-List-Bücherei (GvLB); the two exceptions were first published by Adolf Bürdeke in Switzerland and Leipzig.

Das Geheimnis der Runen (The Secret of the Runes; GvLB no. 1, 1908), the work translated here, is both a brief summary of the intellectual world of List, as realized in the years between 1902 and 1908, and an introduction to the rest of his work. The runes became the cornerstone of List's ideology, and no other work so clearly and simply outlines his ideas on them.

Die Armanenschaft der Ario-Germanen (The Armanism of the Aryo-Germanic People; GvLB nos. 2a–2b, 1908 and 1911) is a two-volume set that outlines the great principles of Armanism, its social history and organization, as well as its cosmological conceptions. The second volume also contains the most pointed use of contemporary racist ideology that List would publish in this series.

Die Rita der Ario-Germanen (The Rita of the Aryo-Germanic People; GvLB no. 3, 1908) represents a mys-

tical delineation of Germanic law, in the cosmic as
well as the political realm. The term *rita* is obviously
borrowed from Sanskrit *ṛta* or *rita*, "cosmic order."
This work also contains a fairly detailed account of
the "Holy Feme" (or "Vehme") as it was understood
by contemporary *völkisch* occultists.

*Die Namen der Völkerstämme Germaniens und
deren Deutung* (The Names of the Tribes of the Peoples of Germania and their Interpretation; GvLB no.
4, 1909) represents the application of List's mystical
theories concerning *kala* (see p. 77ff.) to the many
tribal names of the Germanic peoples which have survived in Roman histories, etc.

*Die Religion der Ario-Germanen in ihrer Esoterik
und Exoterik* (The Religion of the Aryo-Germanic
People in its Esoteric and Exoteric Aspects; 1909 or
1910) is a discussion of the Armanic theories of astrological lore, theology, and numerology.

*Die Bilderschrift der Ario-Germanen: Ario-Ger-
manische Hierogyphik* (The Pictographic Script of the
Aryo-Germanic People: Aryo-Germanic Hieroglyphics; GvLB no. 5, 1910) is one of List's most unique
and fascinating mystical explorations. In this volume
he interprets all sorts of graphic signs and symbols—
including runes, sigils, and symbolic animals—and
then applies his theories to the esoteric symbolism of
heraldry. This is the most sophisticated delineation
of ideas first presented in *The Secret of the Runes* (see
p. 81ff. of the present text).

*Der Ubergang vom Wuotanismus zum Christen-
tum* (The Transition from Wuotanism to Christianity; 1911) is concerned with a central theme in List's
thinking: the (more or less) smooth transition between the pagan and Christian religions. This theory
(many elements of which are perfectly legitimate) allows for the pagan reinterpretation of Christian customs, festivals, names, and so forth, based on the idea

that these were originally heathen (Wuotanist) features that only received a Christian veneer. Thus the pagan ways have, according to List, survived the centuries more or less intact, and are only in need of correct reinterpretation in order to make them living Wuotanist realities again.

It was three more years before List's next, and most comprehensive, study appeared. *Die Ursprache der Ario-Germanen und ihre Mysteriensprache* (The Primal Language of the Aryo-Germanic People and their Mystery Language; GvLB no. 6, 1914) is the encyclopediac presentation of List's complex linguistic theories, based on *kala*. This work actually represents the raising of the tradition known as "folk etymology" to the level of an arcane science comparable to cabalistic number theories. (See p. 69ff. below for a sample of these techniques.)

The disruptions caused by the Great War caused an indefinite delay in the publication of List's last volume of investigations, which was to be entitled *Armanismus und Kabbala.* In fact, by the time the Master died in 1919 the manuscript had still not been prepared for publication, and so it was never made public. Some rumors have it that the work was stolen, others that it was merely kept secret by members of the HAO. This was to be List's great work of magical correspondences. It would have also further developed the mystical history of the way in which, according to List, *Armanen*-wisdom found its way into Judaic mysticism and Renaissance humanism.[32]

The works of Guido von List continued to be reprinted, and the Society flourished until the late 1930s, when it fell under the general suppressions exercised by the National Socialist regime of "Greater Germany." Of course, List's works were read, studied, and collected by the Germanophilic Nazis—most of the copies of List's works to be found in academic

libraries in America bear the stamp of the Reichsführer ss Bücherei and/or that of the Ahnenerbe. (For
further information on the Ahnenerbe, see fn 50.) It
would seem that after the contents of these libraries
were confiscated and sent to America they were sub-
sequently distributed among American (especially "Ivy
League") universities.

THE IDEOLOGY OF GUIDO VON LIST

VIRTUALLY all of the main points of List's ideology are touched upon in this initial volume of his studies. For the sake of analytical clarity, I shall divide the elements into three categories—the cosmological, the sociological, and the mystico-magical (categories of which the Master himself might have approved).

The Cosmological

By "cosmological" I intend to convey the idea of objective trans-human reality—those cosmic processes that List viewed as eternal and heedless of the existence of man. In this category of ideas, List appears to have three main principles:

1. the bifidic-biune dyad *(zweieinig-zweispältige Zweiheit)*

2. the trifidic-triune triad *(dreieinig-dreispältige Dreiheit)*

3. the multifidic-multiune multiplicity *(vieleinig-vielspältige Vielheit)*

Actually, it seems that from these three principles, once they are completely understood from List's viewpoint, all his other principles, conclusions, and mystical interpretations could be derived or deduced.

Armanism is to a large extent based upon paradoxes, seeming contradictions. This is clear in the
formulations "bifidic-biune" and "trifidic-triune," that
is, two-split/two-in-one, three-split/three-in-one. Such
terminology seems reminiscent of early Christian
theologizing over the nature of the Trinity, but List
is going in other directions with those paradoxes.

A derivative principle of the bifidic-biune dyad is
the idea that "matter" is actually solidified or con-
densed "spirit" (see p. 46ff. below). It therefore follows
that there is no essential difference between "spirit"
and "matter"; the only difference lies in the circumstances or conditions in which this singular essence
finds itself. However, List seems quick to point out
that this *condition* also has reality and cannot be ignored. Ultimately, List comes to terms with this paradox by claiming equal validity for both extremes, and
by seeking a balance between them. (See for example
his criticism of "Buddhism" on p. 88 below.)

He insists on the necessity for "spiritual" development, but is equally insistent upon the necessity
for material anchors—the body, the race, nature, and
so on—in order to maintain this spirituality in reality.
And finally List sees both categories as basically the
"same thing."

This balancing factor is also found in the cosmological process itself in the trifidic-triune triad. Whereas
the former principle was rather linear and static in
structure, the threefold process is cyclical and dynamic. The three balances the two.

The most important corollary of the trifidic-triune
triad is found in one of List's most often repeated
formulas: arising–being–passing away to new arising
(Entstehen–Sein–Vergehen zum neuen Entstehen).
This formula is used to indicate List's notion of eternal evolution and return in a cyclical pattern, with
each cycle building organically on the previous one.

Here, we see birth–life–death/rebirth repeated in an organic model of the cosmos into eternity.

Ultimately, all of List's important concepts in the sociopolitical and mystico-magical spheres can be derived from these two basic principles of a spiritual/material dyad in which neither is "superior" to the other, and the evolutionary threefold force of the eternal cycle.

There is also identified a "multifidic-multiune multiplicity," a concept by which List tries to synthesize the virtually unlimited valences of manifestation in the natural/organic world into a coherent wholeness. Here, List approaches a conclusion similar to that of current holistic thought, in which multiplicity is reconciled in a similar way, not with "unity," but rather a "wholeness" model. This allows for genuine multivalence in manifestation without necessarily having to judge one form to be superior to or prior to another.

The Sociological

More than perhaps any other contemporary occultist (with the possible exception of Lanz von Liebenfels), Guido von List concerned himself with "sociological mysteries"—that is, the occult aspects of the origins of the social and racial order—and the magical ways in which to renew the "lost knowledge." Historically, List thought in patterns which should be familiar to many readers of occult literature and that are relevant to the revival of archaic religions such as "wicca," "druidism," or "Odinism." It was his general contention that the practices and beliefs of the Armanen were not wiped out by the Christians but rather were incorporated into the structure of Christian tradition—and thereby survived. Besides this "upward drift" of Armanic lore into the establishment religion, there was also a "downward drift" in which high mystical Armanic principles were encoded in simple folk customs, as for example in the shapes and names of baked goods (see pp. 98–104 below). The result is a traditional environment in which all of the profound secrets of the ancient *Armanen* can still be read in everything from the Catholic liturgy, to medieval literature, to simple folk customs, to Gothic architecture. In truth, there can be little doubt that all of these areas contain some degree—some greater, some lesser— of indigenous pre-Christian tradition. One has but to look at the hagiographies of German saints (e.g., that of Saint Oswald—apparently Wodan canonized),[33] or our own Christmas and Easter traditions to see the degree to which pagan lore and custom were adopted into Christian practice and belief. However, List's methods of uncovering these occult facts differed from that of the modern historian of religion or folklorist in that List first used his "visionary powers" to deduce the general ideas and then would "read" these principles into whatever he might confront. In this way he saw exclusively Germanic (and Aryan) traits in the evidence he investigated.

According to List, ancient Germanic society was arranged in three castes or classes: 1) the intelligentsia (*Lehrstand*), 2) the military (*Wehrstand*), and 3) the peasantry (*Nährstand*). These were identified with the tribal divisions given by Tacitus in chapter 2 of his *Germania*, that is, the *Herminonen* (*Armanen*), *Istvaeonen* and *Ingvaeonen*, respectively. All classes originally grew from the basic farmer-class, so all belonged at least in part to their stock. However, there was little doubt that the intelligentsia—the kings and priests of the nobility (*Armanen*)—were the true powers in the society.

In all this, List could easily be basing himself on Indian practice, bolstered, of course, by the Eddic lay *Rígsthula*, which gives a mythic basis for the origin of the social classes in the north. The theology proposed by List was also tripartite with various triads, such as Wuotan-Wili-Weh; Wuotan-Donar-Loki (Caspar-Melchior-Balthasar [!]); or Freya-Frouwa-Helia, all of which were actually interpreted as figures representing the birth-life-death process. As far as the archaic reality goes, List had a good deal to work from. It was his wish to reestablish a society based on agrarian principles ruled by a hierarchized and enlightened order of *Armanen*.

The racial theories of List were largely borrowed from the Pan-German nationalists around him and from his younger colleague Lanz von Liebenfels. Armanism might be said to be positively racist in that it steadfastly promotes the interests of the "Aryo-Germanic" people over all others—but List seems to have had virtually nothing original to say in opposition to non–Aryo-Germanic peoples. While it cannot be denied that List was a doctrinaire racialist of his time, efforts to show that this was his primary motivation seem misleading.[34]

The Mystico-Magical

The most important mystico-magical tools for List were the runes. By means of his runic knowledge he could read virtually all the "suppressed" symbols and signs of the past. His particular runic system, which he seems to have at least in part innovated himself, enabled him to interpret runically every graph, glyph, name, symbol, icon or image put before him. This amounted to a mystical system in which sound-symbols were correlated with geometrical shapes.

Beyond the basic correspondences between sounds and runic shapes, List added the refinement of a system he referred to as *kala*[35] (see p. 77ff.). In this system, each runic sound is put through a threefold permutation in order to yield its hidden meanings on three distinct levels—the levels of arising, being, and passing away to new beginning. These were also interpreted by List as the exoteric, esoteric, and Armanic levels of understanding. That things not only had a "hidden meaning," but that this occult significance was everywhere threefold, was one of the principal articles of Listian mysticism.

Nowhere is the dynamic synthesis among List's "dyadism," "triadism," and "multiversalism" more clear than in his theories concerning the nature of man, his duty, and his fate. This is touched upon in the final pages of *The Secret of the Runes*. (See p. 106ff. of the present text.)

According to List, the ego *(das Ich)* is a cosmic principle ("the ego in the All as the All itself"). This ego has a certain divine quality, as a "part of God." Therefore, the individual ego is immortal. However, since it, as well as everything else, is "bound" by the three main cosmic principles, the notion of reincarnation or rebirth is made a virtual necessity. But in any case, List does seem to posit that the separate ego or individuality (1) is immortal and (2) does not seek to meld itself with the "undifferentiated cosmos" (as the latter does not really "exist"). Man is seen as a separate agent, necessary to the completion or perfection of "God's work."

It will also be noted that in the final pages of *The Secret of the Runes*, List is encouraging a new "warrior ethic" among his readers, based on ancient Germanic beliefs concerning Walhalla. He maintained that all those slain in battle—or who died "for their ideals"—would return to earthly lives to continue the struggle to final victory. This, according to List, is the esoteric secret of the mystery of Walhalla.

A certain paradox seems to arise from List's idea that the individuality is a free entity and the simultaneously held idea that the "unique will" of this individuality *must* be the same as the "will of God"—

that is, that the recognition of God's will is the *duty* of the individual.

Guido von List was basically a seer. But he was a "prophet" of the past as well as of the future. One of his most important prophesies of future events concerned a formulation he called *"der Starke von Oben"* (the Strong One from Above).[36] At first this might seem to be a prophesy of a coming savior or leader, but List's mysticism took him in another direction. According to him, in an article published in 1917,[37] "the Strong One from Above" would be the collective spirit of those killed in battle during World War I as they were reborn and again came into active life as young adults. Based on astrological calculations, he predicted that the fateful year for the manifestation of this spirit would be 1932. At that time, those killed in 1914 would be eighteen years old in their subsequent incarnations.

Der Meister also used his visionary powers on the past, of course. Before he developed his elaborate systems of esoteric investigation, he was intuitively looking into the distant past of his native countryside. These visions resulted in his early efforts in "mystical journalism" and his early "historical" novels. Actually, his later esoteric investigations were corroborations of these more intuitive early forays into remote antiquity. To criticize his methods from a scientific point of view would be all too easy. It would seem more honest simply to classify List as an occult seer who first used predominately intuitive methods and then developed more regulated arcane techniques to arrive at deeper readings of the same underlying mystical principles.

Sources of List's Ideas

WHEN we come to discuss the "sources" of Guido von List's ideology we are faced with a complex patchwork of influences which List was able to synthesize into a unique mystical view. It cannot be shown, as it has been done with the Theosophists and Anthroposophists,[38] that List plagiarized many of his writings from previously written material. His formulations are unique and constitute an original mystical synthesis. However, that does not negate the fact that List was as much a product of his era as he was to be a shaper of the future. It seems that the influences on List's ideas came primarily from three sources: Germanic mythology and folklore as understood in the mid- to late nineteenth century; Theosophical (and proto-Theosophical) occult ideology, including Indian "theosophy"; and Pan-German political ideology, including the racial theories current within it.

Although List was basically a neopagan, and had been one from an early age—as is seen in the reported vow made when he was fourteen to build a temple to Wuotan—he seems nevertheless to have absorbed a fair amount of Christian sentiment. The "catechism" he wrote in 1898 shows the remnants of this, as does his general attachment to the outer forms of Christian (especially Roman Catholic) symbolism. It seems to be a general characteristic of representatives of the

Ariosophic stream of thought—which is essentially either heterodox/Gnostic or outright neopagan—to be unwilling or unable to reject totally the Christian mythos. It is usually preferable simply to "Aryanize" the mythos.[39] Actually, the works of List indicate that he was not as solidly in this camp as Lanz von Liebenfels. Although he occasionally uses biblical quotes to illustrate a point, he never makes a great deal over proving an original unity of Armanism and Christianity. For List this connection would have come in the historical epochs when each was engaged in the "corruption" of the other.

Germanic mythology and lore were List's primary sources of inspiration, coupled directly with his experiences with nature. In the story about his youthful vow, List himself gives us one of his early sources: the *Wörterbuch der Mythologie*, by Wilhelm Vollmer. Cited as other authors with whom List was likely to have been familiar are Felix Dahn, Wilhelm Jordan, Joseph V. von Scheffel, Robert Hamerling, and Gustav Freytag,[40] all of whom wrote neoromantic fictionalized accounts of Germanic antiquities and the medieval world.

As far as nonfiction studies of Germanic mythology are concerned, it is probable that he was familiar with Wilhelm Reynitzsch's *Über Truten und Trutensteine Barden und Barden-lieder, Feste, usw.* (1802), F. J. Mone's *Geschichte des Heidentums in nördlichen Europa* (1822–24), J. Ludwig Uhland's collection of essays on Germanic myth (1868), and Karl Simrock's *Handbuch der deutschen Mythologie mit Einschluss der nordischen* (1853). List also, of course, made use of Simrock's translation of the *Elder Edda*. All of these writers produced their studies in a less than scientific atmosphere. Methods for the scientific study of sources of religious history had simply not been fully developed and absorbed during the early nineteenth century.[41]

List must have also been familiar with Jacob Grimm's
Deutsche Mythologie (first published in 1835), the
first great scientific synthesis of Germanic religion.
However, List did not absorb any of Grimm's com-
parative methodology. The second significant academic synthesis of Germanic religious history did not
come until the late nineteenth century with the advent of such scholars as E. H. Meyer, W. Golther, and
P. Herrmann. By this time, List's ideas about the Germanic past had already long been set. Besides, his very
mode of thought was essentially different from that
of the academics. There was actually very little common ground upon which they could meet.

The "high mythology" of the elder Germanic gods
and goddesses was not List's only source of Teutonic
inspiration. The so-called "low mythology" of folktales and folk customs formed an equivalent function
of inspiring him as illustrating his rediscovered Armanic principles. *The Secret of the Runes* provides
numerous examples of this.

It seems most likely that List's original synthesis
of Germanic mythology, his subjective nature worship, and his sense of national identity were formulated at an early date (before 1875) and that most of
the later influences of occult doctrines and methods
did not essentially alter this basic outlook. New influences continued to be assimilated more or less
completely into his system.

Important contemporary influences on the form of
List's system included the ideas and poetry of Richard
Wagner, the philosophy of Nietzsche, and of course,
the occult doctrines of Theosophy and the general
current of mystical and magical thought in which
Theosophy arose.

Both Wagner and Nietzsche functioned as virtual
magi of their age. The influences of Wagner's ideas
penetrated into the artistic as well as social, political,
and religious spheres of European life. His vision of

reincarnation

Brahman - Visnu -
Shiva.

Germanic mythology in the operatic tetrology *Der Ring des Nibelungen* (libretto finished 1853, first performed in its entirety 1876) not only added a new dimension of popularity to Germanic lore, but also recast the roles of many of its mythological figures. Wagner, along with Houston Stewart Chamberlain, also led the way in the attempt to forge a link between the ancient Germanic and Christian traditions. The influence of Nietzsche's *Also sprach Zarathustra* (1883–85) is quite apparent in the opening pages of *The Secret of the Runes* where List speaks of the *ewige Wiederkehr* (eternal return) and of "going under" in order to "rise up" in relation to Wuotan's runic initiation.[42]

It is in the area of Theosophy, however, that we see the greatest single impact on the final form of List's occult vision. Principal among its influences on him were the concepts of Indian theology and mystical racial evolution—both of which Theosophy popularized—as well as the idea of the presence of "hidden masters" and the technique of gaining mystical visions of the remote past. Indian theosophy and philosophy is apparent throughout List's work. His dominant concept of the process of birth-life-death/rebirth, and the linkage of that to gods representing creation-life-destruction seem clearly based on the Indian concepts of the three *guṇas* and the later "trinity" of the Indians: Brahman-Viṣṇu-Śiva, popularly known as the Creator, the Sustainer, and the Destroyer respectively.[43] Indian influence is also clear from List's technical jargon, e.g., *rita* for *ṛta*, or "cosmic law," *kala* for his science of word analysis, *garma* for *karma*. Although the ancient Germanic peoples also had a form of belief in "reincarnation," it seems most likely that List had Eastern ideas to thank for this feature of his system as well.

The general link between the mystical racial doctrine of the Theosophists and the racial ideology of

the later National Socialists has perhaps been somewhat overemphasized in previous popular works by
"occult scholars."[44] It seems more likely that both
grew out of a widespread popularization of Darwinian
concepts that penetrated all aspects of science and
culture in the late nineteenth century. For example,
it seems fair to say that the National Socialist racial
ideology probably owed more to Gobineau than to
Blavatsky. To be sure, in the case of List we have a
figure who was clearly as open to mystical notions as
he was to nationalistic ideology. However, in such
matters Lanz von Liebenfels seems to have taken a
much more active and doctrinaire interest. The belief
in the existence of "hidden masters" was not original
with Theosophy, but it might have significantly influenced List's willingness to lend credence to the
"Tarnhari saga." Also, List probably arrived at his
techniques of conjuring inner visions of the remote
past before Blavatsky's writings had reached him, but
these would surely have bolstered his belief in them.

A later influence on List's mystical ideas was certainly Max Ferdinand Sebaldt von Werth, with his
concepts of erotic magic and eugenics.[45] However, since
Werth's works did not begin to be published before
1897, his ideas may be considered only as secondary
influences in the development of List's system.

Finally, we must consider the influences of Pan-
German nationalism on List's ideas. Pan-German nationalism was essentially a sociopolitical movement
with an agenda that included as its primary goals the
unification of all German-speaking people into a single state and the promotion of the social, political,
and economic interests of those people over those of
non-Germans. This, in and of itself, would seem to
have little to do with List's mysticism. But because
his ideas were based on national traditions, and because he had seen in the very land of his native Lower
Austria a sort of sacred territory, List was naturally

predisposed to the ideas of Pan-Germanism, which were very widespread in his day. In retrospect, it seems that the Pan-Germans and List each had something to offer the other. The Pan-Germans could utilize List's vision of the past, which not only gave the Germanic peoples hegemony over all of central Europe but also painted a heroic picture of them as the bearers of a high religious and cultural tradition—in contrast to Rome. For his part, List found in the Pan-German movement an enthusiastic and influential audience for his work and ideas. In the text of *The Secret of the Runes* there is less overt appeal to these interests than in the volumes on the *Armanenschaft* (GvLB nos. 2a and 2b).

The ideas of Guido von List are to some extent the culmination of long historical and cultural developments (Germanic tradition, Christian doctrine, European romanticism), to some degree the synthesis of contemporary waves of popular thought (Theosophy, Pan-Germanism), and in large part also the product of List's own subjective originality and true mysticism.

THE RECEPTION OF LIST'S IDEAS

THE history of the reception of the ideology of "Meister Guido" can be divided into three periods: before his death in 1919, between 1919 and the end of World War II, and since 1945.

Before 1919, the person most responsible for the spread of Armanism was List himself. After becoming an established figure on the Pan-German cultural scene with his literary and journalistic works (between 1888 and 1903), List had an almost ready-made audience for his mystical investigations. The Austrian Pan-Germans knew well the work of the *Meister* and supported him actively through the Guido von List Society. From this group List's literature quickly spread in popularity among groups with similar nationalistic motivations in Germany. By the time of his death, his ideas were no less well represented in Germany than in Austria. List's writings appealed to two cultural factions that are related on many levels yet whose methods and interests differ significantly, that is, the political faction and the occult faction. The political faction seemed most interested in List's ideas as a way to legitimize their programs—although they too were deeply impressed by the arcane appeal to vital irrationalism which was present in List's system and which often justified their ideas. On the other hand, the occultists seemed most interested in List's theories as they applied to the gaining of mystical knowledge about the past, the future, and the world, and in how his runic system could be used for magical purposes. The practical aspects of List's system seem to have been a closely guarded secret, at least during his lifetime. The Listian lore was closely controlled by the publications of the Guido von List Society itself and by those writers and publishing houses closely associated with it.

During List's lifetime, perhaps the most important development officially outside the GvLG/HAO was the founding of the Germanenorden (Germanic Order) in Germany in 1912. Although the aims and methods of the GO were appreciably different from List's own organizations, the influence of List's teachings was mainly in the runological, historical, liturgical, and organizational areas.[46]

By the time of List's death in 1919, his ideas had penetrated—along with several streams of independent but related ideologies—to a popular level. Defeat in the "holiest German War" had perhaps left the German-speaking world more ready than ever for a mystical solution. In any event, an independent use of List's occult runic theories began to develop after 1919. This seems to have emerged in two distinct undercurrents. The first is more obvious and might best be described as *völkisch* occultism. Members of this current generally belonged to the nationalist cause politically, but expressed themselves more readily in the occult genre than in the strictly political genre. Rudolf John Gorsleben and Werner von Bülow generally published works similar to those of List in that they were primarily "historical" and mystical and gave very little indication of how the system was to be used practically. However, two early writers who did expound on and teach practical rune-magic were Friedrich Bernhard Marby (1882–1966) and Siegfried Adolf Kummer (1899–?). Both owe their principal knowledge of the runes to List, although Kummer was more open about this than Marby. It may be true, as claimed by his supporters, that the whole concept of "runic gymnastics," or "runic yoga" was original with Marby. All of these writers made clear their sympathies with nationalist causes and—eventually—with National Socialism.[47] The other undercurrent was to be found in the pseudo-masonic magical lodges of contemporary Germany. Principal among these, the Fraternitas Saturni, which was officially (re-)formed[48] in 1928. Although the general program of this lodge was similar to that of other pseudo-Masonic groups active in Germany, it did also include the development of runic occultism and magic, and at some point even declared itself to be an "ariosophic lodge."[49] The exact history of this development is, however, unclear. The FS, along with all such lodges, was eventually banned by the National Socialists.

A certain group of rune occultists were able to ingratiate themselves into the actual structure of the NS regime. The Ahnenerbe of the SS[50] and the "Rosenberg Office"[51] both actively pursued interests in runology. The work of the former often included perfectly scientific runology. However, both employed pseudorunologists and rune-occultists and made use of rune-magical theories in their researches. For the most part it would seem that in these two official bodies the influence of List's ideas was only one among many streams—including established academic runology—which fed what was essentially a combination of scientific and propagandistic interests. The most direct influence of Armanic/Listian ideas on the workings of the NS regime itself came in the person of Karl Maria Wiligut (1866–1946), who was known by the name "Weistor" among Himmler's SS elite gathered at the Wewelsburg.[52] Wiligut was active in the same *völkisch* Austrian subculture as List, having published his first collection of epic poems, *Seyfrids*

Runen, in 1903. Although heavily influenced by Listian ideas, Wiligut also had a measure of "mystical originality." From 1933 to 1934 he wrote several articles and poems in the periodical *Hag All AllHag/Hagal,* published by the "Edda Society." He composed these under the pseudonym Jarl Widar. It was mainly through Wiligut that Listian ideas were put into effect within the elite Wewelsburg SS community. Furthermore, it is known that Himmler himself not only was interested in such ideas but avidly collected the Armanic literature.[53] The establishment of this "official NS runology" under Himmler, Wiligut, and others led directly to the need to suppress the rune-magical "free agents" such as Marby.

A combination of the policies of the NS regime and the disruption and death caused by the war itself led to a drastic decline in interest in runes and things Germanic in many European occult circles. After 1945, the Listian rune-lore was passed along through three channels: the old structure of the List Society, independent rune-occultists (often with "reformed" ideas regarding their *völkisch* nature), and the initiates of the Fraternitas Saturni (some of whom had a special interest in rune-magic).

Ten years after the end of the war, two rune-magical works of differing backgrounds were issued, both indebted to Guido von List. In that year, 1955, Karl Spiesberger wrote *Runenmagie,* which made use of the Listian eighteen-rune row, and Roland Dionys Jossé published *Die Tala der Raunen: Runo-astrologische Kabbalistik,* which is dedicated to Käthe Schaefer-Gerdau (Protectoress of the Edda Society, 1924–39).[54] Spiesberger was an initiate of the FS (where his magical name was Frater Eratus), and his work seems to represent a synthesis of Saturnian gnosis and Listian Armanism. In addition, rune-magic continued to be employed in the magical curriculum of the FS, which was officially reformed by its original Grand Master,

Gregor A. Gregorius (Eugen Grosche) in 1957. Works by independent rune occultists, such as Jossé and Marby—who after being released from Dachau again took up his runic and astrological work—continued to appear in the 1950s.

It was not until the late 1960s that the actual Listian heritage was reactivated. In 1969, the Guido von List Society was renewed through contacts between Adolf Schleipfer and the still living last president of the Society. The old system was reinvigorated by the new, younger leaders Adolf and Sigrun Schleipfer, who also brought the HAO to an unprecedented level of activity. In recent years they have even begun reprinting the Master's works for a new generation of *Armanen*. In modern German occultism, the Listian system still reigns supreme. Spiesberger's books continue to be in print, new literature in the system appears occasionally (e.g., Werner Kosbab's *Das Runen-Orakel*, 1982), and now Guido von List's works themselves have found a new outlet.

Outside the German-speaking areas, List's influence has been less direct. A number of books on rune occultism have recently been published in English, but most seem to have little tradition of any kind behind them. One notable exception is Edred Thorsson's *Futhark* which, although it adopted the twenty-four-rune, or elder futhark, as its magical basis, does show the marked influence of twentieth-century German occultism—most especially that of List and Spiesberger.

On Translating List

The writings of Guido von List pose a special problem for the would-be translator. This problem essentially lies in the nature of the Listian *kala* mysticism, which is largely based on the phonetic similarities between words as a way to discover occult connections between the concepts underlying those words. In the occult work of List we have what amounts to a mystical system based on wordplay and pun. This, of course, presents enormous problems in translation. If words and phrases were merely translated for their semantic content—the normal procedure—the actual hidden meaning that List was striving to show through sound would be lost. In many instances I have had to use archaic English words in order to show the phonetic connection which is explicit in the German, while on other occasions I have simply had to provide either the original German words or English translations of them in square brackets for this purpose.

Throughout the book, List provided footnotes which either were intended to clarify some point in the text or which refer to one of his other works where the subject is more fully discussed. These notes have been translated and placed at the bottom of the page where the reference occurs and are marked by a progressive series of symbols, beginning with an asterisk. My own notes, by contrast, are numbered consecutively throughout the introductory material and main text of *The Secret of the Runes* and are printed at the end of the book. Within the text itself, List's parenthetical remarks are placed within parentheses, while mine are within square brackets.

THE SECRET OF
THE RUNES

DEDICATION

The content of your letter delighted me very much!
What you have rediscovered and brought to light is
of the greatest interest. —Whatever "official science"
says about it is unimportant. As Dr. Alfred Russel-
Wallace says, science always opposes the discovery of
new Truths, and it is wrong every time! —The true
scholar may say this as well!

Brünn: 4 November 1902
Friedrich Wannieck MP

To the Right Honorable Herr Friedrich Wannieck!
Most honorable sir and friend!

Most honorable sir and friend, I notified you early in
November 1902, that during the months that my eyes
were bandaged due to the cataract operation it would
be impossible to begin to work mentally on my intended unraveling of the secret of the runes, but at
that time—previously unperceived Laws of Generation and Evolution belonging to our Aryan people, of
its emotion, intellect, speech, and writing, came to
me. When I reported this to you, you were gracious
enough to congratulate me by letter on these discoveries. It is from this letter that I permitted myself to
extract an important sentence to serve as a word of
dedication for this book and at the same time as an

introduction for the entire series of works containing my further investigative discoveries.

Above all, I have your encouraging interest to thank, honorable sir and friend, that I can give myself over to research and am able to dedicate myself to these almost unlimited areas of interest. If I may be allowed, let me dedicate this first publication in the series of my research results to you, most honorable sir and friend, as one of your farsighted works which has grown to maturity.

> In highest appreciation,
> Your constant admirer
> Guido von List

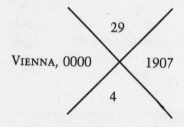

VIENNA, 0000   29   1907   4

Up until now, much too little attention has been paid to the script of our Germanic ancestors—the runes. This is because everyone has begun from the false and baseless assumption that the Germanic peoples had no script of any kind, and that even their writing signs, the "runes," had been imperfectly patterned after the Latin uncial script. All this in spite of the fact that Julius Caesar clearly reported on the account books of the "Helfetsen" (not Helvetier) and their writing, which was supposed to be comparable to the Greek script.

Without attempting to give evidence here of the great antiquity of the runes, which have doubtlessly been found on bronze artifacts and pottery shards, it must be mentioned at this time that the "runic-futharkh"* (Runic ABC) consisted of sixteen symbols in ancient times. According to the *Edda*, in the "Rún-atáls tháttr Ódhins" it consisted of eighteen such signs. With these symbols anything could be written because the Teuton did not know "v" or "w" or "x", nor "z", nor "qu." And neither did he know "c", "d", nor "p." "V" was rendered by "f" (fator = father); "v" and "w" originated from "u", "uu", "uo", or "ou"; "x" from "ks" or "gs"; "z" was probably pronounced but it was written with "s". "Qu" originated from "kui" or "gui", "c" from "ts", "d" from "th" (thorn). "P" developed from "b", until later it obtained its own rune, as did other sounds which gradually received their special runes, so that soon they numbered over thirty.

If you wish to trace the linguistic stems back to the root words of the primal Germanic language, and then follow these further back into the seed- and primal-words of the original Aryan language, you must always write the stem words in runes—or at least have this means of writing in front of you. In this way you may find the correct root, and in this endeavor the name of the rune itself will be an important aid.

Actually each rune has—similar to the Greek alphabet—a certain special name, which is at the same time the *bearer* of the root-word as well as the bud- and primal-word. Here it should be noted that the runic names are unisyllabic words, and are therefore root-, bud-, and primal-words. To this rule only the runes "hagal," "gibor," and "othil" make—seeming—exceptions.

---

*The designation "futharkh" is based on the first seven runes, namely: ᚠᚢᚦᚨᚱᚲᚺ (or ᚺ) it is for this reason that the proper name is not futhark—as it is generally and incorrectly written—but rather "futharkh" with the "h" at the end. For more about the basis of this see GvLB no. 6, *Die Ursprache der Ario-Germanen und deren Mysteriensprache*.

Because the runes have particular names and these names are unisyllabic words, it is self-evident that the runes—in distant days of yore—had the function of a syllabic script, actually a hieroglyphic system. This is because primal Aryan, like every primal language, was unisyllabic, and only in later times was it contracted to an alphabetic script, when the structure of the language proved the hieroglyphic or syllabic script to be too cumbersome.

Now that the runes have been recognized as word-symbols of the prehistoric age, the question as to the abode of the other word-symbols not contained in the runic futharkh becomes quite consequential. Even if a symbolic word-script were extremely poor, which the script of the Aryan language was not, it would need to make use of many more signs than the mere thirty script-glyphs. In fact, [the Aryan script] pre-scribed many hundreds of symbols, and an exceeding number of written signs, as the basis of a highly elab-orate, wonderfully systematic and organically con-structed hieroglyphic structure, whose existence no one before today has considered. As unbelievable as it may sound, these ancient hieroglyphs, rooted far back in the pre-Christian primeval age of Teuton- and even Aryan-dom, stand in full bloom today. They pur-sue their own science, which is still practiced today, and their own art, both of which have their own par-ticular laws and stylistic tendencies. This system has a rich literature as well, but without—and this is the tragicomic aspect—without the guardians and con-servators of this art and science having any idea what it is they are cultivating and developing!*

Because there were, and still are, many hundreds of runic symbols, their exact number has still not been finally determined. However, out of this mass only

---

*For more details as to this: GvLB no. 5, *Die Bilderschrift der Ario-Germanen*.

about thirty came into use as letters in the sense of our modern writing symbols. So at this time, two main groups result from these script symbols, the "letter-runes" and the "hieroglyph-runes," both of which were preserved in their unique ways, and both of which went along their own special paths of development after the separation had been completed. All of these symbols were runes, but today only the "letter-runes" carry that designation, while the "hieroglyph-runes" from this point forward were not recognized as actual script symbols. Because of this differentiation they will be referred to as "holy-signs" or "hiero-glyphs" from now on. It may be noted that the word "hieroglyph" was already important in early Aryan as "hiroglif,"* and it already had its meaning before the Greek language ever existed.

The "letter-runes," which, for the sake of brevity, shall henceforth be referred to simply as "runes," halted their development and retained not only their simple linear forms, but also their unisyllabic names. On the other hand, the "holy signs" were continuously developed on the basis of their old linear forms and were eventually formed into refined and richly constructed ornamentation. They also underwent many alterations in their nomenclature as the concepts which they symbolized, and still symbolize today, were expanded and perfected along with the language.

The mythic lay "Rúnatáls-tháttr-Ódhins" (Wuotan's Runic Wisdom [lit., Tale of Ódhin's Rune List]) of the *Edda* knows the eighteen runes as "script symbols"; however, they still preserve their heritage as "holy signs" in the same sense as the later "magical characters" or "spirit-sigils" (not seals!). Here, the interpretation of that magical song is offered that on its basis the true runic secret can be further unraveled.

*Concerning the primitive Aryan word h-ir-og-lif, see further details below.

No other lay of the Edda gives such clear insight
into the original Aryan philosophy concerning the relationship of spirit to body, of God to the All—and
through Aryandom brings forth so meaningfully into
consciousness the recognition of the "bifidic-biune
dyad" [*zweispältig-zweieinige Zweiheit*] in the mi-
crocosm and in the macrocosm—as does the "Hávamál" and the "Rúnatáls-tháttr-Óðhins" included in it
(verses 139–165).

The perpetually and progressively evolving "ego"
["*Ich*"] always remains through the eternal alteration
from "arising" to "being" and through this to "passing
into nonbeing" which leads to a new "arising to future
being"; and it is in such an eternal evolutionary alteration that Wuotan, like the All and every individual, eternally remains. This "ego" is indivisibly bound
to the spiritual and physical, to the bifidic-biune dyad,
and is constant and immutable. In this way, the
"Hávamál"—the "Lay of the High One"—portrays
Wuotan in an exhalted mysticism, as the mirror image
of the All, as well as of the individual.

Wuotan lives in the human body in order to go
under;[55] "he consecrated himself to himself,"[56] and he
consecrates himself to "passing away" in order to rise
anew. The nearer he feels himself coming to the moment of his "passing away towards new arising"—his
death—the clearer the knowledge grows in him that
the secret of life is an eternal "arising" and "passing
away," an eternal return, a life of continuous birth
and death. This knowledge only completely comes to
him at the moment of the twilight, when he sinks
into the "*Ur*"[57] out of which he will arise again. In
the moment of twilight (death) he gives one of his
eyes as a pledge for higher knowledge. However, this
one eye remains his property even though it has been
pawned. It is recovered after his return out of "*Ur*,"
at his "rebirth," for it is actually his "body," while
his other eye, which he has retained, is his "spirit."

The "physical eye" (actually the body itself) that he
had only temporarily given up—but which remained
his own property—reunifies itself in the moment of
its return out of the *"Ur"*—upon rebirth—with his
other "spiritual eye" (his spirit). However, the primal
knowledge created out of Mime's Well remains his
property, the property of the All; it is the sum of the
experience of thousands of generations, which is preserved and transmitted by means of scripture. Thus
Wuotan's knowledge is exhalted in death, he enriches
it with the draught from Mime's primal-Well, as well
as with the Volva of the Dead and Mime's Head;* he
only appears to divide himself from the physical
world—to which he also belongs in apparent physical
nonbeing—for he truly forms the "biune-dyad" as that
which is spiritual and that which is physical, the indivisible biunity. He cannot divide his own "day-life"
from his "night-life" (death). However, in the "night-
life"—in apparent nonbeing—he wins the knowledge
of his eternal life. This guides him in eternal change
through the transformations from arising through being
toward passing away for a new arising throughout all
eternity. By recognizing that he becomes wise, and by
means of his own life, which was consecrated to death,
he found the knowledge of the world's fate, the solution of the riddle of the world, which "he, eternally,
will never make known to a woman or girl."[58] And
so he is himself, Wuotan, and simultaneously the All—
as certainly as every ego is also a non-ego, or "All."

---

*Mime = memory, knowledge. "Primal-Well" = the mystery
of the All-arising, All-being and All-passing away toward new
arising. "The Volva of the Dead" = the Earth Goddess, Death
Goddess, who preserves the "soul-less bodies" in the cemeteries,
while the "disembodied spirits" go to Walhalla or to Hel. "Mime's
Head" = the Head-Knowledge, that is, the primal knowledge of
arising, being, and passing away to new arising of all things. These
are the three levels through which Wuotan "became wise," i.e.,
attained All-knowledge, and went through the mystery to true
knowledge.

Thus each individual ego, each person, makes the same
transformations for itself through the same levels of
perception by which the understanding and deliver-
ance of every individual is assessed as the spiritual
treasure (not as dead cognitive memories). He does
not lose it even in death, and he brings it back again
when he returns to the world of men in his next incarnation.*

For these reasons each individual "ego" has (for
itself!) its own conception of the spiritual circumfer-
ence of the idea behind these terms, according to its
own "spiritual treasure." Therefore, among millions
of living persons, no two individuals can be found
whose conceptions of divinity are exactly the same—
in spite of all dogmatic doctrines—and so too, no two
individuals are found who have the same conceptual
understanding of the spiritual essence of a language
and its words—both in its details and collectively.

If such is still the case today, in spite of the fact
that other languages have not attained the richness
of our language, how much more must this have been
true in primeval days when the vocabulary was still
a small and insufficient one, and when the seers and
wise men had to wring ideas symbolizing expressions
out of the still limited language in order to be able to
set similar conceptions free, as they themselves conceived them in their spiritual vision. They were forced
to support their speech with physical motions—the
later "magical gestures"—and to enforce it with certain symbolic signs, which were thought of as "whis-
pering" ["raunend"], i.e., conveyors of meaning, and
so they were called "runes" [Runen]. The mysticism
of Wuotan's runic science says all this in the Eddic

---

*We call this "spiritual treasure," which the reborn person
brings into the world, "natural gifts," "talents," or "born genius";
he has a more agile spirit, which comprehends everything faster
and easier than others, others who are animated by a less agile
spirit, and this heightened agility is just that "spiritual treasure."

"Song of the High One," which portrays Wuotan's sacrificial death, and which reminds us of the mystery of Golgatha in more than one respect.

At first, the lay introduces Wuotan himself speaking, after which the skald, who conceived the lay, becomes the speaker and the song is ended. However, the lay begins thus:

> I know how I hung on the wind-cold tree
>   nine eternal nights,
> wounded by the spear consecrated to Wuotan
>   I myself consecrated to myself—
> on that tree, which hides from every one
>   the stead from which its roots grow.
> They offered me neither bread nor mead;
>   then I bent myself down peering;
> with a lamenting shout the "runes" became known to me,
>   until I sank down from the tree.

After further explanatory strophes, the song presents characterizations of the eighteen runes with mystical interpretations. When these strophes are paired with the names of the runes they enlighten us in a very special way and essentially provide the solution of the "secret of the runes." The following verses precede that characterization of the runes, after which the skald goes immediately to the actual runic songs:

> Before the creation of the world was Wuotan's knowledge,
>   Whither he came, thither he returns;
> Now I know the songs as no other men,
>   and as no princely woman.

ᚠ   fa, feh, feo = fire-generation, fire-borer, livestock [*Vieh*], property, to grow, to wander, to destroy, to shred [*fetzen*].

The first promises to help helpfully
   in the struggle and in misery and in every difficulty.

The root-word "fa," which is symbolized as the
"primordial word" in this rune, is the conceptual
foundation of "arising," "being" (doing, working, ruling), and of "passing away to new arising"—and so of
the transitoriness of all existence and therefore of the
stability of the "ego" in constant transformation. This
rune conceals, therefore, the skaldic solace that true
wisdom only lives for the evolution of the future,
while only the fool mourns over decay: "Generate
your luck and you will have it!"

ᚢ ur = *Ur* [i.e., "the primordial"], eternity,
primal fire, primal light, primal bull (= primal generation), aurochs, resurrection (life after death).

I learned another, which people use
   who want to be doctors.

The basis of all manifestation is the *"Ur."* Whoever
is able to recognize the cause [*Ur-sache* = "primal or
original thing"] of an event, to him the phenomenon
itself does not seem to be an insolvable puzzle—be
this fortunate or unfortunate—and therefore he is able
to banish misfortune or increase luck, but also to recognize false evil and false luck as such. Therefore:
"Know yourself, then you will know all!"

ᚦ thorr, thurs, thorn = Thórr (thunder, thun-
derbolt, lightning flash), thorn.

A third I know, which is good to me
    as a fetter for my enemies
I dull the swords of my opponents
    neither weapon nor defense will help him.

The "thorn of death' is that with which Wuotan put the disobedient Valkyrie, Brunhild, into a death-sleep (cf. Sleeping Beauty et al.), but in contrast to this it is also the "thorn of life" (phallus), with which death is conquered by rebirth. This threatening sign surely dulls the opposing weapon of the one going to his death, as well as the force of the powers of death, through a constant renewal of life in rebirth. Therefore: "Preserve your ego!"

os, as, ask, ast = Ase [i.e., one of the Æsir], mouth, arising, ash, ashes.

A fourth still I know, when someone throws
    my arms and legs into fetters:
as soon as I sing it, I can go forth,
    from my feet fall the fetters
    the hasp falls from my hands.

The mouth, the power of speech! Spiritual power working through speech (power of suggestion) bursts physical fetters and gives freedom, it itself conquers all conquerors, who only gain advantages through physical force, and it destroys all tyranny.* Therefore: "Your spiritual force makes you free!"

*In the struggle for existence, the people [Volk] who always remain lasting winners are those who develop themselves with the preservation of their moral force. With the disappearance of morality, higher spiritual and intellectual rank is also lost, as history—the "Final Judgment"—will prove.

R rit, reith, rath, ruoth, rita, rat [rede], roth [red], rad [wheel], rod, rott, *Recht* [right], etc.

A fifth I heard, if from a happy flight
a shot flies into the host;
however swiftly it flies, I will force it to stop
if I can only catch it with my gaze.

The thrice hallowed *"Rita,"* the solar-wheel, the *"Urfyr"* (primal fire, God) itself! The exalted introspective awareness [*Innerlichkeitsgefuehl*] or subjectivity of the Aryans was their consciousness of their own godliness, for "internity" is just "being-with-one's-self," and to be with one's Self is to be with God. As long as a people possesses unspoiled their entire original "internity" as a "natural people,"* it also has no cause to worship an external divinity, for an external divine service bound by ceremony is only made obvious when one is not able to find God in one's own innermost being, and begins to see this outside his "ego" and outside the world—"up there in the starry heaven." The less internal the person is, the more outward his life becomes. The more a people loses its internity, the more pompous and ceremonialized its outward manifestations become—in the character of its government, law, and cult (all of which will begin to emerge as separate ideas). But they should remain one in the knowledge: "What I believe, is what I know, and so I also live it out." For this reason, the Aryan

---

*The "people as a natural people" is not being in a savage condition, for uncivilized "savages" live in the bondage of the most horrible "shamanism." The "people as a natural people," on the contrary, stipulates a high level of culture, yet free from any kind of false sophistication.

divine-internity is also the basis for a proud disdain for death among the Aryans and for their limitless trust in God and in the Self, which expresses itself gloriously in the "Rita," [cosmic order, law] and which has the fifth rune as its symbolic word-sign. Therefore, this rune says: "I am my *rod* (right), this *rod* is indestructible, therefore I am myself indestructible, because I am my *rod*."

Y ka, kaun, kan, kuna, kien, kiel, kon, *kühn*, [bold], *kein* [none], etc.

A sixth is mine, if a man hurts me
    with the root of a strange tree;
the ruin he threatened me with
    does not hurt me but consumes him.

The "world-tree" Yggdrasill* serves in the narrower sense as the Aryan tribal tree, beside which the tribal trees of foreign races are seen as "foreign trees." The runic concept "kaun," "kunna" (maid, e.g., in [the name] Adelgunde) demonstrates the feminine principle in the All in a purely sexual sense. The tribe, the race, is to be purely preserved; it may not be defiled by the roots of the foreign tree. If it were nevertheless to happen, however, such would be of little use to the "foreign trees," because its "foreign scion" would grow to become its raging foe. Therefore: "Your blood, your highest possession."

＊ hagal = the All-hedge, to enclose; hail, to destroy

*For the interpretation of the concept of Yggdrasill, see p. 72

A seventh I know, if I see a fire
   high around the housing of men
however wildly it may burn, I will bring it to rest
   with taming magical songs.*

Hagal!—Introspective awareness, the consciousness
to bear his God with all his qualities within himself,
produces a high self-condfidence in the power of the
personal spirit which bestows magical power, a magical power which dwells within all persons, and a
power which can persuade a strong spirit to believe
in it without any doubt. Christ, who was one of these
rare persons—as was Wuotan—said: "Verily, verily,
I say to you, if someone were to say to this stone:
move yourself away!—and he believes in it—then this
stone would lift itself away and fly into the sea."[59]
Borne by this doubt-less consciousness, the chosen
one controls the physical and spiritual realms, which
he contains comprehensively, and thereby he feels
himself to be all-powerful. Therefore: "Harbor the All
in yourself, and you will control the All!"

 nauth, noth [need], Norn, compulsion of fate.

An eighth I have, surely for all
   most needful to use:
wherever discord grows among heroes,
   since I know how to settle it quickly.

"The need-rune blooms on the nail of the Norn!" This
is not "need" [distress] in the modern sense of the
word, but rather the "compulsion of fate"—that the
Norns fix according to primal laws. With this, the

*Fire-magic, still practiced today as "fire-evocations."

organic causality of all phenomena is to be understood. Whoever is able to grasp the primal cause of a
phenomenon, and whoever gains knowledge of organically lawful evolution and the phenomena arising
from it, is also able to judge their consequences just
as they are beginning to ferment. Therefore, he com-
mands knowledge of the future and also understands
how to settle all strife through "the constraint of the
clearly recognized way of fate." Therefore: "Use your
fate, do not strive against it!"

I

is, ire, iron [*Eisen*].

A ninth I grasp, when for me need arises
    to protect my ship on the ocean:
then I will still the storm on the rising sea
    and calm the swell of the waves.

Through the "doubt-less consciousness of personal
spiritual power" the waves are bound—"made to
freeze"—they stiffen as if ice. But not only the waves
[*Wellen*] (symbolic of the will [*Wille*]), all of life is
obedient to the compelling will. Countless examples
of the "ag-is-shield"[60] of Wuotan, such as the "Gor-
gon's Head" of the Athenians, the "Ag-is-helm," all
the way down to the hunting lore and practice of
causing an animal to "freeze"*, and modern hypnosis,
are all based on the hypnotic power of the forceful
will of the spirit symbolized by this ninth rune. Therefore: "Win power over yourself and you will have

*The magic of "making something freeze" in hunting lore and
practice is substantiated as "hypnosis."

power over everything in the spiritual and physical worlds that strives against you."

ᛘ   ar, sun, primal fire, ar-yans, nobles, etc.

. I use the tenth, when through the air
    ghostly riding-women fly:
  when I begin that magic, they will fare
    confused in form and effort.

The "ar," the "urfyr" (primal fire, god), the "sun," the "light" will destroy spiritual as well as physical darkness, doubt, and uncertainty. In the sign of the Ar the Aryans—the sons of the sun—founded their law [Rita], the primal law of the Aryans, of which the earn, or eagle [Aar], is the hieroglyph. It sacrifices itself, as it consecrates itself in a flaming death, in order to be reborn. For this reason it was called the "fanisk"* and later "phoenix." Therefore it is read as a symbolic hieroglyph when an eagle is laid on the funeral pyre of a celebrated hero to indicate that the dead hero rejuvenatingly prepares himself in death for rebirth in order to strive for a still more glorious future life in human form in spite of all the restrictions of the powers of darkness—all of which crumble before the "ar:" "Respect the primal fire!"

ᛋ   sol, sal, sul, sig, sigi, sun, sal-vation, victory [Sieg], column [Säule], school, etc.

*Fanisk: fan- = generation; -ask (isk) = arising, beginning; therefore: Fanisk or Fanisk = the beginning of generation through rebirth. Fanisk later became the phoenix, and thus is the phoenix explained. Compare "Wuotan's Rune-song": "I know that I hung on a wind-cold tree."

An eleventh still I also know in the fight,
    when I lead the dear one:
I sing it into the shield and he is victorious in battle
    he fares hale hither and hale home again
    he remains hale everywhere.*

"Sal and sig!"—sal-vation and victory—[*Heil und Sieg*].[61] This millennia-old Aryan greeting and battle-cry is also again found in a variant form in the wide-spread call of inspiration: "alaf sal fena!"† This has become symbolized by the eleventh sign of the fu-tharkh as the sig-rune (victory-rune): "The creative spirit must conquer!"

tyr, tar, tur, animal [*Tier*], etc. (Týr, the sun- and sword-god; Tiu, Zio, Ziu, Zeus; "tar"- = to gen-erate, to turn, to conceal; thus *Tarnkappe* [cap of con-cealment], etc.

A twelfth I have: if on a tree there hangs
    a man throttled up on high;
    then I write some runes
and the man climbs down and talks to me.

The reborn Wuotan, i.e., the renewed Wuotan who has climbed down from the world-tree after his self-sacrifice, as well as the renewed "fanisk" (phoenix), which flies up out of the ashes, is personified in the young sun- and sword-god, Týr. According to the rule of mysticism, every magical belief moves parallel to

*Upon this is based the "art of Passau," of "making fast," of invulnerability against any blow, stab, or shot. [The city of Passau was renowned for the practice of magic in the Middle Ages.—Ed.]
  †All solar salvation to him who is conscious of power! (able to reproduce).

mythology, in that the mythic pattern is adopted in analogies to human-earthly processes, in order to reach results similar to those given in the myths. While esotericism on the basis of the well-known bifidic-biune dyad recognizes the mystic One in the mystic Many—and therein it sees the fate of All and hence of every individual—in eternal change from passing away to rebirth. As Wuotan returned after his self-sacrifice—which is to be understood not merely as his death, but rather as his whole life—in a renewed body, so also does every single person return after every life in human form with a renewed body through a rebirth—which is equally a self-sacrifice. For this reason, "tar" means to generate, to live, and to pass away—and therefore Týr is the reborn young sun. So too is the twelfth rune at the same time a "victory-rune," and hence it is carved into sword blades and spearheads as a sign to give victory. It shall be said: "Fear not death—it cannot kill you!"

     bar, beork, biork, birth, song,* bier, etc.

A thirteenth I name, I sprinkle the son
    of a noble in the first bath (pre-Christian baptism)
when he goes into battle, he cannot fall,
    no sword may strike him to the ground.

In the bar-rune the spiritual life in the All, the eternal life in which human life between birth and death means but one day, stands in contrast to this day-in-the-life in human form, which goes from bar (birth) through bar (life as a song) to bar (bier, death), and

*bar = song; bardit = folk song. dit, diet, diut, diutsch = folk, deutsch [German].

which is sanctified and charmed by the "water of life" in the baptism. This (day-in-the-)life is bounded by birth and death, and even if destiny has not at once appointed a sword-death for the bairn—he is still exposed to this and many another danger. For in spite of the determination and dispensation of destiny, dark chance* rules, based in the free will of men, and it is against such a maleficent decree of chance that the sacred blessing is supposed to work. The Germanic people did not recognize any "blind fate." They did believe in a predestination in the greatest sense, but they intuitively saw that many restrictions (chance accidents!) stand in the way of the completion and fulfillment of predestination in order to fulfill and steel personal power. Without these accidents, for example, every pine tree would have to be strictly symmetrical in all its parts; one would have to be the same as the next, while in fact no two can be found that are exactly alike, and so too it would have to be in human life; all without difference, uniform and

---

*Chance!—actually there is no such thing as chance, for all events without exception are in the great web of fate—as warp and woof—all well ordered; but what concerns woof (the cross-weave) is even for clairvoyants only visible with difficulty. The recognizable straight warp of the effects of earlier causes, effects that are always in turn other causes that trigger coming effects (which again form causes that trigger effects, in an unending genetic series), is visible and calculable to seers and initiates; however, it is difficult to tell ahead of time the effects of the woof of the fate of other egos or whole groups of them, and to tell when they will touch, cross, or otherwise influence our woof of fate. These work on our woof of fate—which is comparable to the woof in a fabric, like the woof or cross-weave in such a fabric, and because these incalculable influences often suddenly and unexpectedly disturb our own woof of fate, these are called "chance," without, however, having considered a chance occurrence as something irregular or lawless (that cannot be!), but perhaps as something incalculable. The oldest Aryan mystics already recognized this, and therefore portrayed the Rulers of Fate, the Three Norns, as Weavers of Fate, who out of the "warp" and "woof" weave the "raiment of time," i.e., "fate."

equal. For this reason the newborn should be consecrated with the "water of life"* against impending
accidents. Therefore: "Thy life stands in the hand of
God; trust it in you."

ᛚ laf, lagu, lögr, primal-law, sea, life, downfall
(defeat).

> A fourteenth I sing to the gathered folk
>   by naming the divine names
> for all of the Ase [Aesir] and Elven kind
>   I know as well as any.

The intuitive knowledge of the organic essence of
the All, and therefore of the laws of nature, forms the
unshakeable foundation of Aryan sacred teachings, or
Wihinei (religion), which was able to encompass and
comprehend the All and therefore also the individual
in its arising, working, and passing away to new arising. Such esoteric knowledge was communicated to
the folk in symbolically formulated myths, for the
naive popular eye, unaccustomed to such deep vision
and clairvoyance, could no more see the primal law
than the physical eye can see the whole ocean, or the
unschooled inner, spiritual eye the endlessness of life
in the All. Therefore the fourteenth rune says: "First
learn to steer, then dare the sea-journey!"

ᛦ man, mon, moon (*ma* = to mother, to increase; empty or dead).

*For this reason also the Church, in a clear reference to the
water of life, is supposed to use as baptismal water so-called "living water," that is, spring or flowing water, and rejects standing
water from ponds or lakes.

A fifteenth I tell, which Folk-rast the dwarf
   sang before the Doors of Day
to the Ases [Aesir] for strength, to the Elves for might,
   to myself to clear my mind.

In another sense, as in that of the well-known folk-tale, "the Man in the Moon" reveals himself in the fifteenth rune as a sanctified sign of the propagation of the human race. The primal word "ma" is the hall-mark of feminine generation—"mothering"—just as the primal word "fa" is that of the masculine. There-fore, we have here "ma-ter" (mother) just as there we have "fa-ter" (father). The moon mythico-mystically serves as the magical ring Draupnir (Dripper), from which every ninth night an equally heavy ring drips (separates itself), and which was burned with Baldr; that is, Nanna, the mother of his children, was burned at the same time as Baldr. According to mythico-mys-tical rules, however, nights always mean months, and so the "nine nights" mentioned above indicate the time of pregnancy. While the concepts of man, maiden, mother, husband [Gemahl], wife [Gemählin], mar-riage, menstruation, etc., etc. are rooted in the primal word "ma" (just like the concept "moon," with which they are all internally connected conceptually), they nevertheless symbolize individual concepts recon-nected into an apparent unity according to the prin-ciple of the multiune-multifidic multiplicity. So too is the conceptual word for this unity rooted in the primal word "ma" and expressed "man-ask" or "men-isk," that is: man [Mensch]. Therefore—as a concept of unification—the word "man" is only of one gender (masculine), while the derogatory concept belongs to the third stage as a neuter,[62] to which we will return later. The fifteenth rune encompasses both the exo-teric and esoteric concept of the high mystery of hu-manity and reaches its zenith in the warning: "Be a man!"

ᛂ   yr, eur, iris, bow, rain-bow, yew-wood bow,
error, anger, etc.

> A sixteenth I speak to a coy maiden
>   to get me goodness and luck:
> that changes and turns the wishes and mind
>   of the swan-white armed beauty.

The "yr-rune" is the inverted "man-rune," and as
it designates the bow, so too does it present the wax-
ing and waning moon in contrast to the full moon of
the "man-rune," and so in the first instance it refers
to the mutability of the moon, in the second instance
as the "error-rune"—referrring to the lunarlike mutability of the feminine essence, portrayed in later verses
of the "Hávamál" (Rules of Life) in the following way:

> Do not trust the true words of a maid,
> do not trust the woman's true words,
> her heart was shaped on a spinning wheel
> the feminine heart is the home of fickleness.[63]

The yr- or error-rune [*Irr-rune*], which causes confusion, whether through the excitement of the pas-
sions in love, in play, in drink (intoxication), or through
pretexts of speech (sophistry) or by whatever other
means, will perhaps conquer resistance through confusion. But the success of a victory gained by such
means is just as illusory as the victory itself—for it
brings anger, wild rage, and ultimately madness. The
"yr-" or "error-rune" therefore also contrasts with the
"os-rune" (see above), since it tries to force the con-
quest of an opponent with mere pretext instead of

with real reasons. Therefore, it teaches: "Think about the end!"

      eh, marriage [*Ehe*], law, horse, court, etc.

A seventeenth helps me with a lovely maid,
    so that she will never be able to leave me.

The seventeenth, or "eh-rune" plays off against the sixteenth. While that one warns against frivolous transitory love affairs, the "marriage [*Ehe*]-rune" confirms the concept of lasting love on the basis of marriage as the legal bond between man and woman. This is symbolically indicated by a later "eh-rune" in that the "laf-rune" (see above) is doubled in it (ᛇᛚᚨᚠ= ᛗ ᛃ), therefore symbolically saying: "two bound together by the primal law of life!" Marriage [*Ehe*] is the basis of the folk, and therefore "eh" is again the concept of law, for according to an ancient legal formula marriage is the "raw-root" [*Rauwurzel*], that is, the law-root of the continuance of Teutondom. Therefore: "Marriage is the raw-root of the Aryans!"

Between the seventeenth and eighteenth rune the skald included the following verse:

These songs will be, to you, Loddfafnir,
for a long time well-nigh unlearnable,
rejoice, if you experience them;
take note, if you learn them,
use it, if you understand them.

After this interlude-strophe, he begins with the mysterious eighteenth rune which follows as he again lets Wuotan himself speak:

卐 or ⊕ or 卍 , fyrfos, hook-cross.

The eighteenth I will eternally never
    tell to a woman or maid;
it forms the best end to the lays—
    which only One of All knows,
except for the lady who embraces me in marriage
    or who is also a sister to me.*

In this eighteenth song, the skald again recedes from view; he lets Wuotan sing and speak in order to indicate that this highest knowledge of the primal generation of the All can be known and comprehended uniquely and alone by the nuptually bound divinities of the biune-bifidic dyad of united spiritual and physical power, and that only these, uniquely and alone, understand the thrice-high-holy secret of constant generation, constant life, and uninterrupted recurrence, and are able to perceive the mysterious (eighteenth) rune of these.

However, certainly worthy of note is the fact that the eighteenth rune which is actually present is a— doubtlessly intentionally incomplete—fyrfos, and that it harkens back to this sign in both name and meaning—without, nevertheless, exhausting it. In this the intention of the skalds to guard vigilantly the fyrfos as their exclusive innermost secret, and as the sigil of that secret, can be seen. Only after yielding to cer-

*Wuotan's wife "Frigga" is at the same time his sister, a proof that in antiquity incestuous marriages, of which there are numerous examples in mythology and history, were common.

tain pressures did they reveal another sign which partially replaced the fyrfos.

This sign, which can to a certain extent be seen as
a "substitute" eighteenth rune, is:

ge, gi, gifa, gibor, gift, giver, god, gea, geo,
earth; gigur, death, etc.:

"Gibor-Altar"*—God the All-Begetter!—God is the
giver, and the Earth receives his gifts. But the Earth
is not only the receiver, she is also in turn a giver.
The primal word is "gi," or "ge"; in it lies the idea
of "arising" (to give), but it also indicates "being" in
the idea of the gift, and "passing away to new arising"
in the idea of go-ing. This primal word "gi" or "ge"
can now be connected to other primal and root words,
a few examples of which follow. In connection with
the primal word "fa" as: gifa, gefa, gea, geo, it indicates
the "gift-begetting" earth, and with "bar" or "bor"
(burn, spring), the "gift-burn" God. As "gi-ge-ur" (the
gift goes back to "Ur" [primal existence]), in "Gigur,"
the "gift-destroying" frost-giant, who becomes a per-
sonification of death and later of the devil, appears
to be named. By the idea word "gigas" (gi-ge-as: the
gift goes out of the mouth [as], out of the source) the
fiddle [Geige] is understood. This is the old skaldic
magical instrument of awakening which introduced
the song, and since "song" (bar) also means "life," the
fiddle was one of the many ideographs (hieroglyphs,
symbols) of rebirth, and it is for this reason that it is

*"Gibor-Altar" is still contained in the place-name "Gibral-
tar," a name for which the derivation from Arabic "gibil tarik"
is impossible as can be. "Gib-(-o-)-r altar" was a *Halgadom* (sanc-
tuary) consecrated to "God the All-Begetter" by the Vandals at
the southern extreme of Spain.

often found in graves as a sacred gift. Therefore it is
not necessarily so that the dead man in whose grave
a fiddle is found was a fiddle player. "Flutes and fid-
dles" enticed people to dance, to the excitement of
love, and were therefore banned by the Church—with
its ascetic temperament—because they served as
magical instruments to arouse the human fyr (fire) of
love. So the Church replaced the Wuotanic symbol of
awakening with the Christian symbol of awakening
"the trumpet of judgement." The personal names
"Gereon" and "Geretrut" (Gertrud) are rooted in the
primal word "ge," meaning rebirth, and the hieroglyph of this, the "Head of Gereon," appears as an
equilateral triangle made of three human profiles. But
this Gereon is, in turn, the god incarnate in the All
as the All-, World-, or Human-spirit. And for this
reason the meaning of the "ge-rune" is closest to
that of the "fyr-fos." The difference between the
two interpretations lies in the fact that the idea of
the "ge-" or "gibor"-rune seeks exoterically to approach the comprehension of the idea of the divine
from below upward—in a certain sense from the
level of humanity outward—while the explanation
of the fyrfos seeks knowledge of God esoterically
in the innermost level of man himself—and finds
it. Thus it is known, as the spirit of humanity, to
be unified with God from the standpoint of the
concept of the "bifidic-biune dyad," and it will attain certain knowledge from inside out, as well as
toward the inside from the outside. Here again the
exoteric and the esoteric are clearly distinguished,
and the fyrfos is recognized as an esoteric secret sign
of high holiness, which is represented exoterically by
the "ge-rune." So, while the exoteric doctrine teaches
that "man emerged from God and will return to God,"
the esoteric doctrine knows "the invisible cohesion
of man and divinity as the 'bifidic-biune dyad' "—and

so it can be consciously said: "Man—be One with God!"

Thus in the Eddic song "Wuotan's Rune-Knowledge" (Rúnatáls tháttr Ódhins) the skald interpreted the individual runes—in concealed forms—and implied the "magical songs" (invocatory formulas) connected to them, without actually communicating them—thus preserving the skaldic secret—but he revealed enough that their sense can be rediscovered.

He could confidently conclude the "Rúnatáls tháttr Ódhins":

Now have I ended the high song
   here in the hall of the High-One,
needful to the earthly, not to the giants
   hail to him, who teaches it!
   hail to him, who learns it!
   of the salvation, all you listeners,
   make good use!

*   *

*

With this, the skaldic rune poem and its interpretation, it has been proven that the runes were more than our letters are today, more even than mere syllable- or word-signs, that is, they were "holy signs" or "magical characters." They were, in a certain way of thinking, something similar to the "spirit sigils" (not "spirit seals"!) of later times, which played a conspicuous role in the notorious "Hellish Conjuration of Dr. Johann Faust." Actually they were nothing less than "collectors" for the purpose of auto-suggestion, "media" for concentrated thought and intensive meditation. The characterization as "holy-signs" is therefore fully justified, as is the other name "runes," that is, the "rowning [whispering], the "secretly speaking ones."

Only after these beginnings did those runes, and a number of others that the "Rúnatáls tháttr Ódhins" does not name, gradually shrivel up into letters in our sense of the word—that is, into empty, inarticulate phonetic signs. The great still-uncounted mass of the other "holy signs" or "hieroglyphs," which were not simplified into insubstantial phonetic signs, but which were rather—as has already been stated—often developed with ongoing elaboration into the most elegant ornamental motifs with the characteristic preservation of the basic lines of their primary forms, and which also expanded their names and symbolic values, formed the Aryan system of hieroglyphs or pictographs which remained a secret of the skalds. Until now, no one had thought to decipher or read them, because no one recognized these widely disparate signs as hieroglyphs.

First it would also do well to ascertain where those—until now silent or in the best case misinterpreted—"holy signs" or "hieroglyphs" are to be found, this in order to prove the context of the special formations of individual signs (corresponding to the kind of the areas in which they are found), and finally to establish through their names the primal-words and ideas that they represent, and from these to form a basis for their decipherment and reading.

However, to know the areas in which these signs are found, that is, to find the arts and sciences which supported these signs and which still support them, some other information must be obtained. The old tripartite division of the Aryans, which doubtlessly has its origin in the intuitive recognition of the evolutionary laws of nature, and whose impetus is surely to be sought in the observation of evolution according to natural laws—from the seed through the bloom to the fruit containing another seed—became the essential imperative of the Aryans and of the Teutonic peoples who emerged from them, including the Germans. Therefore, we find in all institutions of the Aryan peoples, in their religions, mythologies, social levels (provider-class, teacher-class, soldier-class) as well as in their language (the "primal-Aryan"), this ideological classification, which, as already mentioned, actually distinguishes verbal concepts into three levels: a) "arising," b) "being, doing, ruling, working," and c) "passing away to new beginning," so that every kernel-, primal-, root-, or stem-word has a concept in each of these levels. But each individual level again breaks down into tri-level sub-levels with the same tendency, and each of these do the same and so forth, so that every root-word and every stem-word demonstrates at least three, but usually many more conceptual values increasing in this threefold progression. Even modern High German is subject to this primal evolutionary law of the Aryan and Germanic languages, which came about before there was any grammar, and which therefore cannot be determined by grammatical rules—although spelling rules endeavor to obscure these levels of meaning in order to prevent misunderstandings that could arise from the confusion of the concepts. To give an example of this from New High German, refer to the word *Rauh* [raw] or *Rauch* [rough], which in its "arising-level" means "to be raw or rough in contrast to being smooth"; through the figure of speech "to work something out of the raw or rough" it is attributed to the first level, e.g., "rough- or raw-materials," "rough and ready," etc. In the second level, that of "being or governing," it indicates "law and justice" as in "raugrave," [*Rauch-Graf*], "rau-hen," [*Rauch-Huhn*], "rau-tenth," [*Rauch-Zehnt*], etc. In the third level of passing away to a new beginning, the word is characterized by the figure of speech "to go up in smoke" [*Rauch*]; this means the smoke of fire, fog, or frost as a sign of destruction. The newer rules of spelling now divide these three ideas by the way they are written: a) *Rauh* [rough, raw], b) *Rau* [rau], c) *Rauch* [reek, smoke]. Other examples are the word *Rad* [wheel], that is similarly broken up in the orthography and indicates: a) *Rath* [rede, council], as a title and description of activity as that which furthers things, b) *Rad* [wheel], the turning, rate, increase, and c) *Ratte* [rat], the destructive animal. A no less interesting example is the word *Hund* [hound] with its many attendant concepts. The "arising level" also means the all-inclusive or basic, so that we have a *Hund* (also *Hunt*), the car on four rollers used to haul ore in the mines [English: "hutch"]; a measure of cut peat (twenty *Hunde* of peat make a "load"); a measure of grain; a measurement of the field (big enough to sow a *Hund* of grain); the name of the founder of a house or dynasty *(Fidei-Kommis)*, e.g., the "Hounds" of Kuenring; a sign of honor in "hieroglyphics," the "red hound" for the establishment of a law. In the "being level" the term "hound" indicates the well-known mammal. In the "passing away to new arising level" the word "hound" [*Hund*] includes the concepts of stoppage, rot, destruction, death, cf. the "hound" on the whim (whim-beam [*Gop(p)elhund*]), the dragging brake; an instrument of torture used to dislocate the joints, a devil's mask (with names such as hell-hound, sun-hound, moon-dog); a judicial sign of humiliation;* as a term of in-

---

*"Hound, dog" in the passing-away level means "to come down [*herunter* (*hunter*) *kommen*], to decay!" Therefore, condemned men bore a mangy dog to the place of execution as a characterizing symbol. Later this symbolism was expanded: thieves carried a bitch to the gallows, and she was hung beside the thief; the bitch and the thief were both called "*Tewe*" ["bitch"], that was clear. Disturbers of the peace carried a setter [*Bracke*] to the scaffold—*Bracke* is identical with "breaker," as a "peace-breaker" or "law-breaker." The red hound means in the third stage "decayed jus-

sult† as well as a proverb‡. These examples, which could be expanded into the hundreds, prove that even the modern German language is subject to the original law of tripartition, even if modern spelling rules—for reasons of clarity of meaning—make the effort to distinguish the concepts through orthographic conventions. But if one takes these modern words back to their stem-words, one will recognize this tripartition at once, especially when one writes the root- and primal-words—as mentioned at the beginning—in runes, or at least keeps this mode of writing firmly in mind.

During the course of this discussion two words were used, and we referred to the fact that we would discuss their three-leveled interpretation (on p. 45 the Greek word "hieroglyph," and on p. 53 the Nordic word "Yggdrasill"). At that time, it was noted that the Greek word corresponded to the original Aryan word "hiroglif" or "iroglif." Both words can be used as examples of the tripartition of concepts.

The word "hieroglyph" appears in the old Aryan language, as already mentioned, as hiroglif or iroglif and may be divided into three root-words "ir," "og," and "lif," which are based on the three primal-words "ar," "ag," and "laf." These root-words have the following three-leveled meaning:

I. Arising stage: "ir" = beginning. "og" = to eye, see, regard. "lif" = to sleep; concealed life.

II. Being stage: "ir" = to contain an arc, in a circle, iris. "og" = to profit, increase. "lif" = to live.

_____

tice," in contrast to the first stage as "foundation of justice" or "codification of law."

†"Dog" as an insulting name has nothing to do with the quadruped; it indicates a violent, despicable person who wants to bring everything down [herunter (hunter), cf. Hund], to decay.

‡"To go to the dogs" [Auf den Hund kommen] also has nothing to do with our pet, unless it means it is a less valuable draft-animal than the horse, but rather also refers to "downfall" [Herunterkommen (Hunterkommen)] into poverty and decay.

III. Passing-away stage: "ir" = error, confusion. "og" = to separate [*schneiden*] (*orlog* = war: as the decider [*Entscheider*]. "lif" = to conclude; certainty without out doubt.

Out of this, the three levels of interpretation for the word "hiroglif" result as follows: First stage: "the beginning is regarded in the concealed mind"; second stage: "the (knowledge) contained (in the sign) increases the living (knowledge); and the third stage: "confusion cuts off certainty," i.e., whatever is fixed by writing can no longer be confused. The Greek interpretation from *hiero* = "holy," and *glypht, glypho* = "cut into stone," is insufficient. Even if *hiero* meaning "holy" is covered quite well by *hiro* having to do with "the beginning," the second half is wrong, because hieroglyphs were far more often written or painted than carved into stone. But if one wanted to have *glypho* stand for "spiritually deepened," and thereby recognize the sense of "sacrally deepened," then such an interpretative speculation would come quite close to the old Aryan concept.

In a similar fashion the word Yggdrasill is divided into the three root-words "ig," "dra," and "sil," which result in the following three-leveled meaning:

I. "ig" = "I" as shaper, generator, producer, consecration. "dra" = turning generation (trifos), generation of fire. "sil" (sal) = sal-vation.

II. "ig" = (uig, wig) struggle (Viking). "dra" = to drag, carry. "sil" = law, pillar [*Säule*].

III. "ig" = terror, death. "dra" to destroy (dragon). "sil" (zil) = aim, end.

Out of this, three levels of interpretation of the word Yggdrasill (Igdrasil) result as follows: First: "I, generating sal-vation in the primal fire [*Urfyr*]!*, sec-

*Compare the "burning thorn bush" in the Bible, Exodus 3:2.

ond, "warrior of the law, war tree, war-horse," third "aim of terror or destruction, the tree of terror." This explains much that is otherwise not comprehensible, especially the incorrect interpretation of the name as "horse of terror." The World-Ash "Iggdrasil" is the Tree of Life of "Aryan" humanity, their "sacred fire," their "original salvation" (see the burning thorn-bush). It is, however, thought of as living, therefore existing and governing, and for this reason it is the "warrior" [war-bearer]—graphically the "war-horse" of humanity.

Ultimately, it will be the "tree of terror," by which humanity will pass away. But it is also the "wind-cold tree" about which Wuotan sings in the rune-song. For this reason, the designation "World-Ash" is also meaningful, for "ash" is "Ask"—the first man, the primal-father of humanity who bore the same name (the primal mother was called Embla, i.e., "Alder") and "man-ask," "men-isk" [Mensch] = man [human]— has its origins here. However, as "man" signifies the generative, shaping one in the first stage, and in the second stage humanity is indicated as living and existing, so in the third stage the ruined individual—no longer worthy of being called human: "the slut" [das Mensch][64] is scornfully named. "Ask," in and of itself indicates: (1) the beginning of humanity, figuratively the primal-father, (2) the ash, and (3) the ashes and from that: asc-eticism [Askese], destruction of reproduction. Manask or monak is therefore the monk, a word that we also have in Aryan as well as in Latin (monachus), for surely even Latin is derived from Aryan.

Even though these few, and only briefly sketched, examples should be sufficient to indicate the tripartition of all concepts in the Aryan system and their net-like interweaving, nevertheless another example should be taken into closer consideration in order to take up the thread again and spin it out further.

Already on p. 69 above, mention was made of the

tripartition of the folk into provider-, teacher-, and soldier-classes. In this regard it should be remembered that Tacitus and Pliny, and to some extent the Greek traveling scholar of the fourth century B.C.—Pytheas—all already had made mention of a tripartition of Germanic society, which according to their documents consisted of the three tribes—the "Ingaevons," the "Irminons," and the "Istaevons." According to Tacitus, the Earth-born god "Tuisco" (Týr, Zio, the generator) had a son "Mannus" (Menask, man) who generated three sons, namely "Ingvo," "Irmin,"and "Istvo," who are supposed to be the tribal fathers in the familiar three levels of conceptual meaning: "Ingvo" (ing-fo) = (1) perpetuator, maintainer; (2) the young wanderer; and (3) the one who decides in court. "Istvo" (ist-fo)* = (1) the generator, who generates in death, the returning one, the one to be reborn, (2) the continuously existing one, and (3) the one who goes into darkness, submersion. The ending "-ons" in the three tribal names means on three levels: (1) the ancestors, the primal origin; (2) to wander; and (3) to change, transformation, rotation.

Therefore the tribal name "Ingaevons" means: (1) the ones who came forth out of ancestral origin, (2) the wandering young descendants, wanderers, Wandals [Vandals], and (3) the alteration through the judgment of fate.

The tribal name "Irminons" means: (1) the ones who came forth out of the ancestral origins of the solar man, (2) the wandering governors, solar judges, Semanes (not Semnones), and (3) conclusion of opinion by a turn of fate.

The tribal name "Istaevons" indicates: (1) the ones reborn out of the realm of the ancestors, (2) the ones

---

*From this probably comes the Hungarian man's name "Istvan" for Stephen.

constantly wandering, and (3) the ones who pass away through a consequence of fate.

According to tripartition the first level of conceptual meaning serves as the general designation for the "Ingaevons," the second for the "Irminons," and the third for the "Istaevons." But all three designations have their special uses according to the rules of the "trifidic-triune triad," for all three are really but one, that is, the whole indivisible Germanic people.

All of this is based on the fact that all Aryans or Teutons felt themselves to be one folk. On account of this, every individual, be he free-man or king, had to belong to the provider-class in order to prevent this class, as the main class, from being devalued. Everyone had, therefore, to be a farmer, that is "Ing-fo"—an original maintainer and perpetuator of the ancestors. The second class was the intellectually advanced, the intelligentsia, the rulers, the "teaching-class," to which the skalds, the high nobility, and the kings (princes, counts, etc.) belonged—without ceasing to be farmers. It has already been said on p. 56 above that "ar" means the sun and the law of the sun, and the earn, the eagle [Aar] is its symbol and hieroglyph. Therefore a member of the second class was called an Ar-man or Ir-min, namely a sun-man, Se-man.* The Se-mans were the men of knowledge [Wissenden], and from them emerged the skalds—the priests of Wuotan†—or better said their core group was the

---

*Tacitus mutilates this word in "Semnones," just as, for example, Julius Caesar confused and made incomprehensible the folk-name Helfesen or Helfetsen as "Helvetians." The same is true for all Germanic folk- and place-names in Roman or Greek writings, and it would be a welcome task for someone to set these names aright and thereby make them "speak." For names "always say something," they are not empty shells when they are correctly reconstructed. And that shall and must happen!

†Guido List, "Von der deutschen Wuotanspriesterschaft," Das zwanzigste Jahrhundert (Berlin) 4, nos. 2–5 (1893).

skalds, who, as priests and teachers were also the judges—for in those times *"Wihinei"* (religion) was simultaneously science and law. One believed what one knew—or at least intuitively recognized, and lived accordingly. Since the Semans, Irminons, Skalds, etc., were one and the same with the scholars, artists, etc., this second class is the "teacher-class"—in spite of the fact that it too belonged to the farmer-class—and is to be recognized as the root area of the activation of the Aryan spiritual work. Therefore, all original lines of the collective arts and sciences are to be derived from it. However, the skalds must remain the central focus in which all the diverse special manifestations of the hieroglyphics can be unified. The third class, the "soldier-class," the "Istaevons," who are "those who pass away due to a consequence of fate"—is in no way that which we today understand as the military—for all members of the folk were responsible for the common defense—but rather they were the great mass of surplus populace who had to migrate in order to establish new states. There was no personal ownership of land and soil, only familial estates—the elder governed it for his clan, the members of which only had rights of usage over it. If their number became too great for the ownership of land, then the surplus would have to migrate *("hel fesen")*—never to return. They elected a "duke" [= "war-leader"], and he searched for land. Since such migratory expeditions—or colonization efforts—were carried out completely according to *rita* [= cosmic law], the power of the Aryans to found and maintain state structures, recognized by all historians in all times and places, is evident. Throughout the whole world we find these Aryan foundations which are testified to in historical as well as continuing folk-, land-, and place-names of Aryan state establishments—reaching all the way back into prehistoric times.

Because the skalds, as the scientists, maintained

language, art, and science, they were also primarily concerned with scientifically directing the transition from Wuotanism to Christianity,* and to prepare the way for a peaceful blending of the two religions. But this effort was soon disturbed as the second violent period of Christianization broke forth under bloody Karl the Great (Charlemagne)—the Slaughterer of the Saxons. In spite of the fact that the skalds were persecuted and scorned, they collected themselves together and secretly took the German faith and the German law in a concealed manner into the "hidden tribunal" [heimliche Acht] of the "fem" (five) fingers of the sword's hilt—and thus arose the band of the "Holy Vehme." Out of the "Skaldic Order" the "Minne-singer Order" later emerged, as did the "German Builders' Guild" and the "German Heraldic Guild." From all this, in broad branchings, sprang the judicial sciences, poetic arts, linguistic sciences, graphic arts, etc.

Because the skalds, as poets and singers, were also the maintainers and formulators of language—and because it was necessary for them to preserve in strict secrecy the Wuotanism that they took with them underground into the "heimliche Acht" (in order not to be persecuted as heretics), they had to use the three-fold interpretation of words to have their messages delivered—even by messengers—without these or other noninitiates being able to understand the correct interpretation. Through steady skillful practice they reached such refinement in this double-edged type of poetry (called heimliche Acht or kala), that one and the same text could conceal two completely different messages, whose obvious sense (understood by every-

*Concerning this see my essay "Vom Wuotanismus zum Christentum," in the weekly Der Deutsche (Berlin), 1, no. 13 (1904). Compare also my essay "Von der deutschen Wuotans-priesterschaft," in Das zwanzigste Jahrhundert 4, nos. 2–5 (1893). [Ed. note: List also discusses this transition at length in his book Der Übergang vom Wuotanismus zum Christentum.]

one) would actually be secondary, while the concealed sense *(kala)* would contain the only real, secret message for the men of knowledge. However, not all words in such messages served the *kala,* but rather only single words among them. These were distinguished by their initial sounds (alliteration), and were therefore called code-words or passwords [*Kennworte*]. Now, these code-words explained the accompanying text in a completely different direction—usually in the exact opposite direction from the apparent meaning—and in this way they explain many medieval poems that are otherwise incomprehensible. In this hidden Wuotanism we can, however, understand the cause of the strictly guarded "guild secret" of the Minnesinger Order, the Heraldic Guild, the German Builders' Guild, the Vehme, and other bodies that emerged from it. In addition, we can understand the formal richness of their customs of initiation, advancement, and internal association in this way. However, in a very notable way, their secret symbology, which they fixed in the holy signs as "hieroglyphs" and the like, according to the *heimliche Acht* or *kala,* gave a double secret meaning. The interpretation of these hieroglyphs is also twofold, and if one will, threefold, as in the following:

1. The interpretation for the common, uninitiated folk, which is evident in the portrayal—whether in speech, writing, pictures, or sculpture (or even in custom and gesture)—is the same; e.g., a lion, a fox, a bear, a greeting, etc.

2. The lower symbolism or the exoteric, which is usually expressed in the ecclesiastical-clerical understanding or in commonly known, easily understood correspondences, and which in any event was created for the purpose of being offered to the lower grades of the guild (apprentices, journeymen, etc.) as the "lesser light." This is done in order to test their trustworthiness and secretiveness, before the "complete great secret" or "the greater light" can be given to them in

the higher grades (elder-journeyman, master, herald, royal herald, etc.). In this exoteric level, for example, "the lion" indicates "the lion that goes about looking for the one he will devour," or courage, royal essence, etc.; "the fox" points to cunning and craft; "the bear" to strength, etc. The "handshake" greeting (grip) has its secret characteristic by which one is able to recognize the one who is being greeted, whether he is a Fellow or not, and if so, to which degree he belongs. The password would then aurally strengthen the impression gained from his grip and facial characteristics.

3. The high symbolism of the esoteric, the great secret of the *"heimliche Acht,"* the "full light," proceeds from a purely Armanic perspective, and interprets only abstract concepts of theosophical-metaphysical content. It has the ultimate aim to provide a basis for that which was in the beginning blended with the full light, but it is to be introduced with growing intuitive knowledge, gradually dispensing with all symbolic aids and finally being able to base itself on its own intellectual conceptualization. Only then will the hieroglyphs be alive, as they make clearly expressed conceptual interpretations perceptable from flat comparisons. On this esoteric level, the examples of hieroglyphs already introduced may be rendered in the following way: lion = life, law, light, sun; fox = generation (*fas, voss*); bear = birth; also the greeting increased in meaning and even became more secret— for precaution was necessary. Also the code-words of greeting and passwords received another meaning from what they had in the second degree.

If the essence and origin of the Aryan hieroglyphics are now clear, then too their branchings in various areas of use are easy to prove—areas in which use was made of them, and areas in which use is still made today. However, it must be said right from the beginning that the usual interpretations today, without exception, are relevant to the second degree—on the exoteric level. This is because the third degree of interpretation—on the esoteric level—has been lost. But it should also be noted here that this loss is only apparent. The key to the deciphering of the secret lies in the language which we still speak today, and in the tripartite nature of the word-concepts.

In the course of this study, it was discovered that the Skaldic Guild [*Skaldenschaft*] unites within itself the origins of all arts and sciences which are even today in full bloom, and that the skalds were active— already in distant antiquity in considerably pre-Christian times—as poets and singers, as heralds (painters), as master builders (sculptors, stone masons, carpenters), as philosophers and theosophists—as well as judges. They founded and refined their symbolism and hieroglyphics in these branches of arts, sciences, and crafts, and ultimately in the Christian era they handed down their arts and crafts through various developments, which had been taken into the *"heimliche Acht"* along "hidden ways," to the guild-leagues of sciences which had grown out of them. Through the struggles against the Church (witchcraft trials, persecutions of heretics, upheavals during the Reformations) as well as through other upheavals in the "Holy Roman Empire of the German Nation" the majority of the traditions in those bodies were lost, and only disparate remnants of misunderstood formal odds and ends have been partially preserved to the present day, while the soul—the inner life—has disappeared. The same is true of "Freemasonry," which originated from the stonemasons' guilds.

Only in the still-flowering art and science of our ancient Aryan, indigenous heraldry, or science of coats-of-arms, have Aryan hieroglyphics been preserved. But today even heralds know only the exoteric readings of their hieroglyphics. They call them "secret figures" and "heraldic devices," without having a notion of their esoteric legibility.

Medieval and early medieval buildings of Romanesque—or better said old Saxon or old Germanic and
Gothic—styles form a further area of discovery. In
these buildings, hieroglyphs were elaborated into extremely high artistic developments, so that those
structures *speak*, when the hieroglyphs are "read."
And they can convey surprising results.* The revived
contemporary Gothic style, however, had no notion
of hieroglyphs in its tracery, which is only stylized
decoration, and which therefore degenerated into misunderstood forms and symmetries.

No less often do these symbols find their way into
"speaking records," into legal antiquities and pieces
of wisdom, into folk customs, folk beliefs and prov-
erbs, then into alchemy and medicine, into astron-
omy, astrology, and into all disciplines related to the
mystical endeavors of antiquity and the Middle Ages—
right on up to the present day. That many of these
signs were even, so to speak, popularized in the most
everyday utilitarian objects and even determined the
forms of such things is certainly conceivable with
such a widespread tradition. Here, for example, we
only have to mention the forms and names of our
breads and baked goods. In brief, it is not easy to find
an area in the life of the German folk which these
hieroglyphs, holy signs, and symbols do not illumi-
nate. However, for present purposes, only heraldry,
German architecture, and legal symbolism will be
considered.

In the symbolism of heraldry all the runes are abun-

*Compare Guido List, "Die symbolischen Bildwerke am Rie-
sentor der Stephanskirche zu Wien." *Laufers Allgemeine Kunst-
Chronik*, 1889, nos. 9–11. Even if this work still seems uncertain
and tentative (since at that time a complete understanding and
correct use of the key was not yet available to me), nevertheless
it provides a more or less correct reading (at the time more "sensed"
than clearly recognized) of the hieroglyphs, and was only in need
of a clear foundation and minor rectifications.

dantly met with in the heraldic figures. They form
the dividing lines of heraldic devices. Because they
were painted on shields and were calculated to have
a certain effect at a distance, the heralds "tinctured"
the background beside the runic lines with contrast-
ing colors. The colors used also had a definite meaning, and were again dependent upon the rune. The
heralds learned to see the runes and to "blazon" the
shields according to the surfaces defined by the runic
lines, and therein lies the confusion. For example,
they blazon a coat of arms with the "fa-rune": "per
pale, sinister a bar sinister," similarly with a "gibor-
rune": "upper pale rompu, lower pale rompu," "dexter
or sinister fess fracted, beveled or square," "downward
fracted bar sinister," "dexter bend fracted," etc., etc.,
according to the portrayal and position of the rune. A
coat of arms with the "thurs-rune": "per bend with
counter pile," "with counter pile, or with counter
wedge bend," etc., whereby the first two indicate the
"upstanding thorn," and therefore "arising of life"
(phallus), and the last one indicates the sunken thorn,
or the "death-thorn" (cf. Brunhild, Sleeping Beauty).
[See the Runic Table.]

The holy-signs* were developed in even more interesting ways. In the first place, we must discuss the
"fyrfos," [fylfot] which, as soon as the bordering line
of the tinctured fields appeared, was blazoned by the
herald as "quarterly per square," or "quarterly per
wavy," etc. Later, as the figures were being executed
in painted surfaces (and no longer only in linear fashion), the "fyrfos" was also being portrayed as a colored
figure with linear outlines, and was called the "hook-
cross" [Hakenkreuz]. Because the "fyrfos," even under
the code name "hook-cross," was still the "heathen
cross," and thus could bring a herald under suspicion

*"Die esoterische Bedeutung religioser Symbole" by Guido von
List, Gnosis (Vienna), 1, no. 16 (December 1903).

of heresy, the greatest care was taken to conceal its hooks as much as possible in order to make it appear more like the "Christian cross." In this way the many so-called "heraldic crosses" originated, such as, among others, the "gringoly (serpent-headed)-," the "T-square-," the "Jerusalem-," the "arrow-point-," the "botonée-," the "fleury-" (*Deutscher Ritterorden*, Order of the Teutonic Knights), the "moline-," the "bough-gable-," the "mill-spindle-cross," etc. One of the most significant concealments of the fyrfos is probably the so-called "Maltese Cross," which appears to be made up of two opposed hook-crosses in linear fashion, which now form the well-known eight-pointed figure that is painted a different color on the inside (from the field on the outside), and so it took on the appearance of an independent figure; however, this was only intended to feign such a sign. This sign was called "Baphomet" or the "talking head" and was used as evi-

dence for heresy in the Templar trials, and as one of the grounds for the condemnation (1313) of the Templar Order. It was; however, nothing but their "speaking head-sign" (i.e., "main sign" in the sense of the third esoteric secret degree of the Wise mentioned above (on p. 79). The Knights of Malta and the Knights of Saint John, who today still use the same cross, were only able to

avoid a fate similar to that of the Templars by means of heavy sacrifices. But the Order of Teutonic Knights also uses the Germano-Armanist hook-cross in the cross fleury still concealed in the ancient and honored fyrfos—which is descernible to the Wise.

A further very interesting example of a hidden hook-cross is offered by the crest of the Lower Saxon town Bad Pyrmont am Osning near the Porta Westphalia [i.e., on the border of Westphalia], well known for its

mineral waters. It contains two hook-crosses executed on a flat surface. These crosses are superim-

posed in such a way that, of the
underlying cross, only wedge-shaped
parts of the arms and the spreading hooks
can be perceived, so that in its entirety
it gives an impression similar to the
cross moline.

The "ordinances" in heraldry, that is, people, animals, utilitarian objects, etc., are also hieroglyphs like
countless other "heraldic devices"—which cannot be
discussed in detail here—and as such are only legible
according to the third esoteric degree of the *"heimliche Acht"* or the "great secret." Following what has
been said above (p. 79), these always have a concealed
sense and never signify that which is represented as
such. Therefore, in the springtime of heraldry, when
the *heimliche Acht* was still active, these portrayals
never appear formed in a naturalistic way, but rather
are always treated ornamentally in the style so characteristic of the old coats of arms. The picture, be it
an eagle, a lily, a "fire-dog" [= andiron] (*Fyrbock* ["fire-
goat"]), or whatever, never signifies just the object
itself but rather the hieroglyph derived from this object; and it is this too that the artistic ornamental
elaborations are supposed to indicate. An instructive
example is offered by the heraldic earn (eagle), about
which it has already been stated (above, p. 56 and
75) why it is the hieroglyph or device of Aryandom
and of the later German Empire, a hieroglyph which
was already being borne by the Aryans in Asia, e.g.,
Cyrus the Achaemenian, as well as the Pharaohs,[65]
the Greeks, and the Romans. It symbolized the power
of the state and was naturally one-headed. When it
occurred to the Papacy to free itself from the power
of the state, thus beginning the "Investiture Contest,"
the German king put the double-headed eagle on the
imperial coat of arms and thereby said that he was

lord of both forms of law, of the secular law of the state as well as of ecclesiastical law.

The eagle-maiden of the crest of the city of Nuremberg only has meaning when it is addressed by its old name, i.e., *"wipare"*—which would sound like *"weibaar"* ['wife-earn'] today, but which is preserved in the word *"Weberin."** It signifies the female weaver of fate, the "Norn," after which Nuremberg is named, and so it *speaks* as does every—genuine!—old crest. *Wibare*, the Weaver, is, however, at the same time the *"Arkona"* (Sun Lady) as well as the *"Urkona"* (Primal Lady, or Primal Mother, or Ancestral Lady). So in turn, it is the "white lady" about which so many castles and palaces report and which is also at home in the castle of Nuremberg. Also the saga of the "white lady," or the "ancestral lady," belongs to the realm of hieroglyphics, for she is found at places of primeval origins (birth), but never at places of rule or governance (of life).

In any case, all sagas, folktales, and myths according to the third esoteric secret level have special meaning with regard to the place to which they are connected, and they also work to explain the place-names themselves,† and contribute in a completely unexpected way toward the illumination of the primeval history of Aryandom over the whole world, not only in central Europe.

The sculptures on Romanesque (or better said old Saxon or early Germanic) and early Gothic cathedrals and secular buildings—which had been up to now puzzling—find their key in the symbolism of the Ger-

---

Weberin [(female) weaver] = *Webarin* = *Wibarin* = *Weibaarin*. [In Listian code "wife-earn," i.e., "eagle-woman."]

†For more details on this, see "Wien und sein Leopoldsberg," by the author of this treatise, in *Die Entwicklung* (Vienna), 2, no. 1 (1904). A report on the *"kala"* and other *"kala-places"* as well as on the *"verkalte* [i.e., concealed] skaldom" at the locations of pre-Christian "halgadoms" [i.e., sanctuaries].

man building lodges and in this system of "hieroglyphs." (See note on p. 81.) These figures were
continuously being perfected into a richly articulated
ornament right up until the late Gothic and transi-
tional style, and they are even still recognizable in
isolation during the early Renaissance; but later they
are lost track of completely—which happened in conjunction with the decay of the German building lodges.
But even in the traditions of architecture the main
holy signs, i.e., the "trifos" or "vilfos" (actually will-
fos), the "fyrfos" [fylfot] (hook-cross), and the "ruoth-"
or "wheel-cross" [*Radkreuz*], also called the "whisk,"
take on very important meanings in all sorts of ornamentation used in the construction of tracery and
rose windows; the first as the flamboyant trifoil, the
second as the flamboyant quadrafoil, and the third as
the "Saint Catherine's Wheel." The other Gothic hieroglyphs are too numerous to count, but wherever one
looks these will be found in a very special arrangement—proclaiming the "great secret of the *heimliche
Acht*" to the Wise.

The trifoil as the "vil-fos" indicates the "will to
generate," with reference to the creation of the world
as well as to the activization of life. The quadrafoil
as the hook-cross, however, signifies the "all-encom-
passing cross," from "*haag*," "(to) hedge (in)." The
name "hook-cross" is just a code word for "hag-cross";
it symbolizes the god in the All as well as in every
ego, as a "*haag*" (see *hagal*, p. 53). The "wheel-cross,"
which appears in a hidden form as the "Saint Catherine's Wheel," points to the "Judgment of the World"
at the end of time, and so the flags during the Peasants'
War [1525] had wheels on them (the "little wheel
flags")—the peasants wanted to hold court over their
oppressors! The five-angled star, the Vehme-Star, the
Truthenfuss[66] (*truh* = turn, *fuss* = foot) is the hieroglyph of "revolving or turning generation," of "rebirth"—one of the most important articles of faith in

the Aryan religion. In its exoteric interpretation this sign simply says: "return," and was therefore a favorite sign used at hostels and inns, in order to convey the meaning: "whoever is a guest here should come again."

Thus these hieroglyphs are easily carried over into the highest theosophical and metaphysical realms of ideal conception, all according to their functions and dispositions, for they exist in the sphere of everyday life in order to transfigure this life, in order to show that ideal striving and real struggle actually flow into one another as the great mystical "biune-bifidic dyad."

It will already have been noticed that when the main or primeval holy signs were named: "vil-fos," "fyr-fos" and "ruoth-" or "wheel-cross," they also had other names, e.g., "vilfos," "four-fos," "whisk," and even further designations such as "tri-fos," "turn-fos," "three-foot," "triskelion," "four-foot," etc. It can be seen that in order to conceal the esoterically indicated "will," the insignificant "many" [*viel*] was imposed in order to veil the esoteric "tri" [three] (turning, of the turning of the earth and stars, of the whirlwind, of the storm, etc.) and at the same time mystically to indicate the number "three," as well as the number "four" for "fyr." This hidden "fyr" occurs to an uncommon extent in architecture, e.g., in "quartering" [*Vierung*, the intersection of nave and transepts], in the "guide" or "slide" [*Führung*], in the "square" [*Vierege*] (fyroge = fire-eye = god's eye). The last of these earned an important meaning in secret rituals under the code name "tapis" [a carpet] and also "tabula quadrata," which symbolizes "arising," "existing," and "passing away to a new arising." The corner diagonal to that of the middle lamp of existence had no light, for it indicated the northern side, the darkness of corporeal nonbeing which was followed by the new light in the east, the coming rebirth, the new light of arising. Around this "tapis," with its three lights in the

east, south, and west, and its mystical darkness in the
north, the Fellows of the builders' lodges made their
symbolic migrations through the life of the immortal
ego, of the spiritual ego, whose ways lead them through
countless births and an untold number of lives in
human form, toward an equal number of deaths, and
through these into the darkness of the "Primeval"
[Ur], in order to attain to new arising through many
rebirths, to renewed life in renewed human bodies.
These migrations of the immortal ego are, however,
intended to indicate not a circular development, but
rather a continuous rising—like a spiral staircase—
in order to approach the final aim of the highest perfection, of a similitude to God, and ultimately to full
union with God in this spiral form. All hieroglyphs
which indicate the stepladder point to this end, but—
and this is the important thing—*but without ever
losing the real rock-solid foundation which lies firmly
established in the recognized indivisibility of the
physical from the spiritual, and in the acknowledged
"biune-bifidic dyad."* It is in this that the main strength
of the—indestructable!—Aryan religion lies. While
the Aryo-Indian Buddhist acknowledges only the spiritual and disdains the physical (and so by maintaining
his ethnic individuality has lost his political freedom),
and while, on the other hand, the Mediterranean Aryans (Greeks and Romans) acknowledged only the
physical, thereby quickly attaining a high culture and
status as world powers, but (see note on p. 52) through
damage to their moral force lost the culture they had
attained and disappeared without a trace, the central
European Aryans—the Teutonic peoples, including
the Germans—by recognizing the "biune-bifidic dyad"
cultivated the spiritual and physical as inseparable
and coequal—and so they preserved not only their
ethnic individuality but their national freedom as well.
In possession of both of these they were also able to
hold on to their original Aryan Armanendom as a

priestly class in contrast to all other peoples of the earth.

In the symbolism of German administration of justice a great number of such holy signs, symbols, and hieroglyphs are once more found; however, in a much more lively variety of forms than in painting (heraldry) or in sculpture (architecture). This is because they served in matters of law as "speaking attestations" [*redende Urkunden*] (as "verbal and truthful signs"), and as such were placed in opposition to the statements of witnesses and the "living evidence." Therefore they were neither painted nor chiseled nor symbolized in any other way, but appeared in their natural state and therefore attained a very noteworthy meaning in their symbolic-hieroglyphic interpretations. In the administration of justice, too, the old Aryan tripartition is naturally found again as (1) arising or law (*Rita*), (2) the existing, ruling (justice), and (3) the passing away to renewed arising (the court). Because law and justice culminate in the decisive pronouncement of the court (and consequently, as the third level, this provided the final result) the holy sign of the court was the ruoth-cross, rod-cross, or rowel- [wheel] cross which was therefore also known as the Vehme cross, consisting of a fyrfos whose hooks were bent in the circular shape of a wheel rim. As the Vehme cross it appears engraved on the blade of the great Vehme-sword as an equilateral cross enclosed by a circle. At the cross point the letter "V" appears, and furthermore in the quadrants between the arms the letters "S.S.G.G." were engraved. These letters probably displaced the formerly used runes ᚡ and ᚻ ᚷ (doubled), which signified: "Vehme" and the old passwords: "*Strick*" [string], "*Stein*" [stone], "*Gras*" [grass], "*Grein*" [branch?], i.e., "wyd" ["white"] = law; "brick" = secret; "rage" = thunder = doing = ar = right-doing; *greyen* = to uphold; that is: "Through law and secrecy (*heimliche Acht*) right-doing is upheld." In abbreviated form this is: *tue esse, tue gege* (two s's and two g's).

In the *heimliche Acht* or *kala* all this signifies "present in the hidden," which exoterically refers to the watchfulness of the Vehme, esoterically to the omniscience of God as the highest judge. *For this reason the "ruoth-cross" was the symbol of the court, and it is for this reason that the crucifix on the bench of the modern judge should be seen—not as a symbol of religion—but rather as a substitute for the "ruoth-cross."* Wherever the words *"Rothenkreuz"* [red-cross], *"Rothenburg"* [red-castle], or even *"roth"* [red], *"Rad"* [wheel], *"Ratt"* [rat], etc., occur in place-names, there is where there was at one time "marked steads of the Vehme," as, for example, near *Hochroderd* in the Viennese Woods. All "red crosses" that stand in lonely forests were at one time Irminsuls or Roland-columns, i.e., "mark-columns," which designate such "marked steads,"* and all "red courts" were at one time the property of the Wise of the Vehme.†

Therefore "speaking attestations" were—as has been said—opposed to "the living witnesses," and both were therefore considered as equal in German law. They were consequently memorial marks or tokens for the recollection of an *"Urtet"* or *"Urtat"* [original act]; they were therefore pictorial signs, and hence hieroglyphs. Such "living images" include the coif and breast [of a woman], dogs, roosters, chickens, geese, etc.; "speaking images" include eggs, cheese, oats, grains, etc.; while "memorials" (also thought of as speaking) such as stones, hills, graves, trees, straw, twigs, helmets, shields, lances, axes and spurs, memorial coins,

*For basic information about this, i.e., concerning "the *halgadom*," the *"wihistane"* [holy stones], and marked steads at the red cross, see my essay "Vorgeschichtliche Bauwerke im südlichen Bohmen," in *Heimdall* (Berlin) 8, nos. 11–13 (1903).

†E.g., The Red Court in the eighth parish in Vienna (at one time the town of Josephstadt).

gloves, etc., are well known. Mountains, hillocks (*Buk*), columns, rivers, and brooks served as "*Saalen*" [halls]—likewise speaking attestations—and it is from these that we get *Saal*-mountains, rivers, forests, and fields.[67] These "*Saalen*" are not only "borders," but also "holy" (*sal, sul, sil*) and consequently also the target [*Ziel*], the final goal.

The "straw" pulled from the field and handed over to the new owner was the "speaking attestation" of transfer (renunciation) of a property. "*Hal*" is that which is "hale and holy." The one leaving the land therefore gave over the property with all that was hale and holy still attached to it. In the "drawing of straws" the longer straw decides the "lot"—as the "greater boon" [*Heil*]. Even today we say "He drew the shorter one" when one has bad luck. Similarly, the "staff" (sta-fa—standing) of steady generation, i.e., life continuously renewing itself, is a much-used hieroglyph. In the hand of the judge it is the "wise staff" —the guiding staff which guides the law—and so it is therefore white in color, because white (*wit, wyd*) as a color means law. As a "red staff"—in the criminal court—it is the "staff of justice" (right-staff), for red as a color means justice ["right"](ruoth). It is for this reason that the executioner wears a red coat. For the condemned the "staff is broken," i.e., life is broken, just as he has broken the law, and is therefore called a lawbreaker. The staff of the king is of gold. Gold as "ore" designates the descendants; the king preserves living justice for the future. The royal staff is called the scepter, which as "*scipan*," or "*scepan*," means the shaper of justice.* The bishop's staff [crosier] is called the "crooked staff." However, being bent, crooked or turned means an inverted life, i.e., "my kingdom is not of

---

*Therefore those who occupied the courts were called the "*scephan*" = *Schöffen* as "shapers"[68] or creators of justice, and not something like the "scoopers" (as in dipping water from a well).

this earth"; the bishop should, according to this hieroglyph, have no power in secular justice. In the Investiture Contest it was decided otherwise, however.
The "hand" is the sign of ownership, but also of personal freedom. The unfree man might neither give
nor take by his "own hand," but rather only by the
hand of the magistrate; only the freeman had the power
of his "own hand." Only he, as a "genuine proper-
tyholder" might "take something away by his own
hand." From this idea come the expressions "to promise by mouth and hand," and "the magistrate shall
manage the residents." "The bond" [Handfeste, i.e.,
something fixed by hand] is a document or letter ra-
tified by a seal and signature. "The dead hand"—of
the unfree man—is one that can neither give nor take.
(The modern concept "dead hand," referring to clerics,
is not relevant here.) The Vehmic magistrate disposed
with his "left hand." Again we are dealing with kala
or heimliche Acht, for Ling (left) = head; he man-
aged [behandelte] and maintained [behauptete] the
sentence that he shaped. The imperial princes at the
Imperial Diet disposed with the "right hand." "Hand-
clapping" was—as it still is today—a sign of approval.
The investiture of royal jurisdiction without a retinue
upon a man was carried out by the one being invested
kneeling while holding his "flat right hand" in the
"flat right hand" of the king. This was a "ceremonial
handshake." To get to the upper hand means to go to
a higher court. A "chopped-off hand" or "an ax" on
places or on government buildings hieroglyphically
indicates "municipal" or "baronial jurisdiction." The
"hand with a sword" is the hieroglyphic sign of jurisdiction, designating the "supreme censure" or the
highest jurisdiction, and also the seat of government.*
"The gloved hand" indicates the protective jurisdiction, the "civil court." From this we get "the

*The National House in Vienna.

hand-token" [Handmal] as the sign of the court at a
border-stead [Malstatt], be this now a stone, a pillar,
or whatever kind of "mark" [Malzeichen]. "A bloody
hand takes no inheritance," i.e., whoever sullied his
hands with human blood would lose his inheritance.
According to tribal law, it fell to his next of kin. But
also no judge who "judges with a bloody hand," i.e.,
who exerts capital punishment, may take (confiscate)
the property of the condemned man from his heirs.
Therefore: "A life for a life, the property remains
to the heirs, only the horse, harness, gear, and coinage
belongs to the magistrate, and whatever is above
the belt to the bailiff and that below the belt to the
hangman." Much else could be said concerning the
"hand," "handshake," and other "hand signs," but
this should suffice.

The "hat" was the hieroglyph of protection, and
growing out of this, of the lord's justice. It obviously
meant shelter and guardian.[69] At the enfeoffment the
liege and the vassal would grasp each other's hands
inside a hat. This signified that the vassal was under
the shelter [die Hut], under the protection of the liege,
but also that the vassal was ready to aid the liege if
he needed it. The "hat on a pole" (Gessler's hat) is a
sign of sovereignty; the village mayor who came to
the auction of a bankrupt farmer's property entered
the barnyard and stuck his walking stick (staff = life)
in the ground in the middle of the yard and clapped
his "hat" over it. With this action he had taken possession of the farm, by right of his power.

Women swore by "hair and breast": "Ir rise das sol
sin ir trouwe," i.e., her hair (risan = that which grows),
that is her coif, shall be her troth [faithfulness]. The
breast is the sign of nourishment, of wet-nursing, of
mothering, of Minne.* Minne is memory.[70] This is

---

*Minne, Menne, Männe, Manne, Moraminne, Miromanne,
Meremenne, etc. = the woman who nourishes, the wet nurse.

why "hair and breast" is in the saying: "Remember the one who grows"—as a mother of future generations it is her duty to be mindful of, and to stand by, truth, justice, and "Ar." (Female breasts also mean the same thing in heraldry and architectural symbolism, e.g., with the *Wibare* [ar-wife, see p. 85], the "sphinx," etc.).

Here it should still be remembered what was said on pp. 70–71 about the "hound" as a symbol of justice as well as a chivalric sign of shame in order to show how all three levels of the concepts mesh, and how one and the same hieroglyph can be—according to their arrangement—a sign of honor or shame. This has only now been made comprehensible.

However, there also existed yet another foundation of *kala* to which the reader's attention can only now be drawn, because this rule will only be comprehensible from the "hair and breast" example. Above (pp. 68–71) it was said that *kala* secretly indicates the hidden meaning of words on some other level of interpretation, in which the Wise had to be able to recognize the "concealed right sense"—but when the profane hearer perceived and interpreted the word it was only comprehensible according to the listener's level of understanding. Thus there came about many double meanings: *Ar* [sun] and *Aar* [earn, i.e., eagle]; *fos* [fot, as in "fyl-fot"] and *Fuss* [foot]; *fos* and *Fuchs* [fox]; life and lion; birth and bear; *Brake* [setter] and *Brecher* [(law)breaker], etc., are all to some certain extent "direct concealments," while the examples "hair" and "breast" are known as "indirect concealments." Now, indirect concealments are based on a transposition of concepts, such as "tress" or "lock" for "hair," that is, the "collective" for the "singular"; such as "breast" for the "concept of mother-

---

Maan, Mon, Man, Men, etc. = man, moon. See "Man-rune," pp. 60–61.

hood," that is, the "means" for the "end." They stand, therefore, despite the poetic veiling, in very close associations of meaning with the intended interpretations. For us, the difficulty of interpretation comes in because we have to look for this far off from the modern or usual meaning of the words, and often only after many detours can we recognize the interpretation—if ever found—as being one very close to what we sought. In this regard, it should also be pointed out that the interpretation of a word in its kalic sense is never valid as a model for all other cases, but rather each one must be solved independently, even if the solution of one case can be of use as an analogy. The rules valid for such variations just have to be found. Their causes may be discovered in local linguistic customs from the time period in which they originated and in other circumstances; however, in this regard, it may also be noted that even today hard and fast rules without exception are difficult to find. This is because these variations demand free room to play and not narrow limitations. These were living word-pictures shaped from the living language and were felt to be such. This feeling has been lost through overuse. Even today, there is a similar situation with *double entendres* and wordplays which will surely become incomprehensible to later generations for whom the contexts will have become quite strange. In this regard, it must be expressly noted that *"kala"* or *heimliche Acht* is in no way comparable to such wordplays.

A further condition for the correct understanding of these "holy signs," "runes," "symbols," and "hieroglyphs"—and one which may never be ignored—lies in the clear comprehension of pre-Christian ethics, as well as pre-Christian morals. One can never forget that Wuotanism grew out of the intuitive recognition of evolutionary laws in natural life, out of the "primal laws of nature," and that *Wihinei* (exoteric religious system) formed by Wuotanism spread a teaching and

conducted a mode of living based on the laws of evolution. It set for itself a final goal of bringing into
being a noble race, whose destiny it was to be to ed-
ucate itself and the rest of humanity as to the actual
task of human beings. This task consisted of the ex-
tension of the work of God according to the intention
of these laws—that is, to further the constant process
of generation founded on the laws of evolution. In the
recognition of the "multiune-multifidic multiplicity
[*vieleinig-vielspältige Vielheit*] of the All" and in the
recognition of the "eternity of the ego as an individual," which was recognized in all its countless pre-
and post-existences as immortality, the individual
conquered the fear of death and led the consciousness
of the folk, borne along by such a teaching, on another
and a far more certain pathway toward a disdain for
bodily death. This led to spiritual as well as physical
heroism, to Armanism, and to their being the teachers
of all other peoples. Another religious system came
and fought against Wuotanism in that it disdained the
physical and only recognized the spiritual, and igno-
rantly wanted to inhibit the process of evolution, processes that exist—and are therefore desired by God—
the incontrovertible "primal laws of nature." They
intended to overcome the fear of death, by denying
the pre- and post-existences of individual selves [*Ich-
heiten*] in physical being, and in its place taught an
eternal spiritual life divorced from the physical world.
This doctrine would—if it could win lasting influence, which appears out of the question—destroy the
noble race as well as its heroism in the spiritual and
physical realms, and in its place breed a population
of slaves who would be forced to degenerate into the
most dull-witted shamanism—below even the cultural level of the Australian Aborigines—that is, if
the will of God, which expresses itself programmat-
ically in the immutable primal laws of nature, would
ever allow such a thing.

life-denying religious system

Now, because men of our contemporary age are caught up in the ascetic view of a life-denying religious system, but in spite of this cannot deny the primal laws of nature, a distorted morality had to be developed, which spreads hypocritical appearances over hidden actions. This has brought to a head all those outward forms of modern life, whose vacuousness and corruption are now beginning to disgust us. From the side of this "false morality" there developed that which the early medieval Germanic folk still called *situlih*, that is, "true wisdom." This old word has been weakened to *sittlich*[71] in our modern language, and preserved with a completely altered meaning, which roughly translates as "immoral." This teaching, which accorded with the laws of nature, was openly distrusted as a "sexual religion." It hardly needs to be especially pointed out what a healing power just this distrusted "sexual morality" can exercise today, and what it will exercise in spite of everything, for the primal laws of nature are the divine law of primeval (*Ur*) evolution, they are the will of God, and therefore cannot be denied in the long run.

It is, however, precisely from the standpoint of this powerful morality (the "true wisdom" of Wuotanism) that the "holy signs" and "hieroglyphs" must be examined, for Wuotanism lifted women to the level of goddesses, and lifted the procreative act (fyrfos, fa-rune, ge-rune, thurs-rune, etc.) to a sacrament, while later cultural periods—which in a self-satisfied manner fancied themselves to be exhalted over the previous ones—set about to take away the divine status from women, to degrade them to prostitutes, and to profane the creative act of generation as a simple vice. For only a few independent thinkers and their students has it become possible to renounce the learned moral theory, with all its hypocritical asceticism, and all its conventional policelike views that hem in all free thought, and to recognize in the old Aryan sexual morality the truly traditional and true wisdom—which must and will lead our folk to salvation. Therefore, it is only those who will understand and value what is to follow, while the others, according to their inclinations, may be horrified.

Arising, being, passing away to renewed arising is the old Aryo-Germanic primeval three; the fa-rune opens and the ge-rune closes the futhark, the rune row. Every exoteric system of religion, and so too the Wuotanic "Wihinei," recognized "human sacrifice" as indispensible in appeasing the divinity. But these human sacrifices are based on cannibalism, which is still echoed—even if it sounds mythical (exactly!)— in all religions in the form of "blood rituals." Even in the Nibelungenlied[72] it is reported that the heroes in Etzel's [Attila's] burning hall quenched their thirst with the blood of their fallen comrades, and in Der arme Heinrich[73] we get a detailed report of such a blood sacrifice—even if it is one mitigated to the level of a healing ritual. So we are really not all that far away from the times of cannibalism. What we call "execution" today is the last remnant of bloody human sacrifice.* Later, man made the transition from cannibalism to the eating of animal flesh, even if the "faith" still demanded human sacrifice—prisoners of war, criminals, and in the absence of these, slaves. Only later did the representative animal sacrifice, and still later the representative bread sacrifice—whether in the form of sacrificial cakes or the host is irrelevant—take its place. Esoteric schools already recognized at an early time (see pp. 46–48) that the entire life-span in a human body signifies a sort of sacrifice, but only very gradually could they cause the symbols

*"Die Sage vom heiligen Gral und deren mythologischer Ursprung," by Guido List, Bellitr. Lit. Beilage der Hamburger Nachrichten, June–July 1891, nos. 26–29. "Die schwarze Maria" by Guido List, Deutsche Zeitung (Vienna), no. 7022 (30 July 1891) and Der Bund (Bern), 2 April 1893.

to be transformed into bloodless ones, and to rescue from that "faith" the people who would have been sacrificed by substituting "sacrificial cakes" which were formed and named after the intended victims. Even today during the consecration the priest says: "This is my true blood, this is my true flesh!" He has to repeat this during each sacrificial operation in the most ceremonial manner in order to convince his faithful that the "substitute sacrifice" is the will of God. In spite of this there occurred as late as the seventeenth century so-called "black devil's masses," or "coercive masses" which included actual human sacrifice.*

If such things were happening in Christian—relatively recent—times, how hard might it, and must it, have been for the skalds to succeed in replacing bloody sacrifices with bloodless ones. That they were successful is, however, shown by the forms and names of bread still in use today, which harken back far into the pre-Christian ages. But here it should not be thought that they had been able to suppress bloody sacrifice completely, for attitudes and customs that are so deeply rooted only die out very slowly, and always revive again wherever the old faith—without esoteric leadership—sinks into superstition, sorcery, and fetishism, such as it turns out to be in witchcraft and the lore of the witches' sabbath.†

---

*Examples of excessively hideous "black masses," which promoted the development of the most unrestrained imagination, are found in *Historie de Magdaleine Bavent, religieuse du monastère de sainte Louis de Louviers,* etc. (Paris: Jacques le gentil, 1652) and in "*Médecins et Empoissonneurs,*" by Dr. Legue, who used the records of the trial against Abbot Guibourg, a scandalous trial in the time of the Roi Soleil Louis XIV which compromised the highest aristocracy in such a way that it had to be hushed up as quickly as possible. These examples are said to be typical even for later times right up to the present day, as such spawns of madness celebrated their orgies in the mysteries of Satanism, and are even thought still to celebrate them.

†See my series of articles: "*Zauber und Zauberglaube,*"

These "substitute sacrifices" were so-called "sacrificial cakes" or "sacrificial breads," and they symbolized the "human body" in whose stead they were brought to the gods as sacrifice. Later other shapes also symbolized "animal bodies" and still later even symbols or holy signs of the gods themselves by which the sacrificer, who consumed the sacrificial food, thought to sanctify himself.

Here we already have the three basic designations: "bread," "cake," and "loaf."[74] "Bread" (ber-od; ber = to bear, to generate; od = spirit, intellect, wit; therefore an artificial product generated by wit and intellect) is considered one of the first products of the human gift of innovation, and certainly the first artificially prepared food, which is already indicated in the name. "Cake" ([Kuchen] kok = to prepare; an = origin; therefore, mother-cake, to which the idea of birth is attached = symbol of the feminine) was already the first representative sacrificial baked good substituted for a woman. "Loaf," which in some dialects is still called "loaf-bread" [Lab Brot] (lab = life, body [Leib]of the human, life) is such a representation, which is indicated by the navellike impression in the middle of the "loaf."[75] As a "loaf," "bread" was designated as being suitable as a sacrifice. Now, however, there occurs in addition to these an absolutely incomprehensible quantity of bread and pastry forms, which appear to be explicable only according to what has been said above. The "Wecken" (a breakfast roll)[76] is the male member as the "awakener" of procreation, symbolically designating the man in order to substitute for him as a sacrificial offering. The "Baunzerl" represents femininity in exactly the same sense. The

Deutsche Zeitung (Vienna), 1890–1892. Among these: "Das Hexenwesen," in no. 7241 (26 Feb. 1892) and "Der Hexenprozess," in no. 7282 (7 April 1892). The other essays are in nos. 6531, 6620, 6703, 6880, 6999, 7053, 7093, 7184, and 7297.

"Stangel" [salted bread-stick] is the staff (*sta-fa; sta* = standing, steady, *fa* = procreation; therefore: steady procreation) and designates continuous procreation, while the salt (*sal* = salvation, hale) strewn and baked on it makes this form of bread recognizable as a "talking image" of the constant salvation of procreation. The *"Kipfel"*[77] (*cyphen* = bowed, therefore also called *"Hörndel"* [croissant]) is the "moon-horn," and it has already been shown (pp. 60–61) how the moon is associated with femininity. The crescent moon as the *"Wendehorn"*[78] is, however, also the rune of Freya, who promotes childbirth. A skaldic circumlocution which explains the *Kipfel* and *Hörndel* as the "golden horseshoes of Wuotan's steed which the lucky find in the grass" is merely *kala* and again relates to the childbearing principle. "In the rough of life the lucky ones find the mother of their children, the one who prepares the future." The *"Semmel"*[79] (*se* = sun, spirit, soul; *mel* = meal, to mill or marry[80]) is divided into five parts, and therefore represents the *"Fem-* or Vehmstar" or the "Witches' Foot," the pentagram (see p. 81) and symbolizes rebirth. The maternal, physical binds (mills or marries) itself to the spiritual in continual return to rebirth. The *"Bretze"*[81] [pretzel] (*bere* = to bear; *tze* [*tse, se*] = to make, and therefore conducive to birth) is in the form of the "bar-rune," and not, as is falsely interpreted, in the shape of a wheel. The "pretzel," also called a *"Fasten-bretze"* [fasting pretzel] (*fas* = generation; *ten* = to withhold), was therefore a symbolic, holy food, which proclaimed the warning to refrain from sexual intercourse during pregnancy. We may not regard such symbols in a limited way as divine coercion or as coercion exercised through religious proscriptions; they were much more a well-thought-out and effective means of educating a naive folk-spirit, and as such are the founding pillars of later hygenic proscriptions upon which our society still rests today. The *"Kringel"* [little ring, cracknel]

(*kar* = to enclose; *ringel* = ring; enclosed in the ring; or also from *krinc* = circle, i.e., the orbit) is the course of the sun, of life, of the eternal return. The "*Krapfen*,"[82] "*Kroppel*," or "*Krapfel*" was the sacrificial pastry which was offered and consumed in the second half of the great festival of beginnings, which we call Yule, or Holy Nights [*Weihnachten*]. The first half of the festival, from the twenty-fourth of December to the thirtieth of December, stood for the creation of the world and for the past; the thirty-first of December was the "cleft in time," which divided and bound past and future—the "now"; while the second half, from the first of January to the sixth of January, was the celebration of the mystery of the creation of man (generation) and of the future. This then lined up with "*Fasching*"[83] (*fas* = generating; *ing* = continuous, descended from something; see "Ing-fo-", p. 74ff.) Furthermore, the *Krapfen* (*crap* = to tear out or to tear down; *fen* (*fe, fa*) = generation) served as a symbol of the awakening of life and was therefore the food eaten at Fasching. The "*Fladen*" [flat cake] (*Osterfladen*, *Osterflecken*) was the Easter pastry and the Easter sacrifice. *Fladen* means "pure" and is still preserved in the woman's name "Elsfleth." *Ostern* [Easter] (*os* = mouth [vagina]; *tar* = generating) is the festival of the marriage of the Sun-god with the Earth-goddess, the festival of the regeneration of natural life; the pure virginal Earth-goddess enters into the bonds of marriage with the Sun-god—this indicates the name and form of the *Fladen*.[84] The "*Stritzel*" or "*Heiligenstritzel*" [holy-*Stritzel*] was the sacrificial bread of the great festival of the dead, that today we celebrate in Christian form as All Souls' or All Hallows'. It is braided together out of three long pieces of dough in a manner similar to braiding a person's hair. The name of this sacred bread (Middle High German "*struzzel*" from *struiza*, "stra," "stoh" = empty, to part with, to take away; and therefore straw [*Stroh*] as the empty

stalk, from which we get the "crown of straw" as a
sign of shame; the "straw-maid;" but "*stro*" is also
return, and therefore "straw widower" [grass wid-
ower][85]—so that here we have a picture of death and
the coming rebirth) therefore hieroglyphically gave
reassurance that we will see our dead loved ones again
after rebirth. It is also for this reason that it has the
symbolic tripartition of the tresslike form. The "*Vier-
fussel*" [four-footer], a favorite Yule pastry, that is even
today frequently chosen as a Yule-tree decoration, is
in the shape of the hook-cross [swastika] formed by
two S-shapes crossing each other, and it indicates—
even if today it is unconscious, like almost every other
pastry shape and name—the ancient holy fyrfos. The
"*Beugel*" [bowed one] is a subordinate form and subordinate name of the "*Kipfel;*" the "*Mohnbeugel*"
[poppy-bread] as a Yuletide food points to the "moon"
and "man" as well as to *Minne* = memory. Now, we
should also call to mind the "*Lebzelten*" [gingerbread
tent] of the "*Lebkuchen*" [gingerbread cake]—an old
Germanic sacred pastry. "*Leb*" comes from the root-
word "*laf*," from which the word *Laib* [loaf] is also
derived, and now means in the first, arising level:
loving, generating, etc.; in the second, being- or becoming level: life, body, loaf, liver, etc.; in the third,
the passing away–toward new arising level: death,
fermentation, curdling, etc, from which we get the
"lee-barrow" = grave mound or mountains of the
dead. The gingerbread tent therefore also has three
meanings, as can be recognized even today in the things
to which it is dedicated. It is a symbol of love and of
symbolic declarations of love in its forms as a "child
in swaddling," "rider," "cock-rider," "heart," etc., the
forms of which are, of course, hieroglyphs. As festival
pastries, so-to-speak as "pastries of life," it has the
most various forms, such as "fishes" (good-luck fishes),
etc., while it is recognized as a pastry for offerings to
the dead in the shape of a round or rectangular (*fyroge,*

see p. 87) tent. This latter form refers to the symbolic journeys through birth, life, dying, death and rebirth.* The name "tenting" [*Zelten*] (from "tent" [*Zelt*], i.e., "*tel*" is generation, hence *Telt*, the generated, the earth, and *Tellus*, the Earth-god), however, points to birth as well as to resurrection.

In addition to these, however, one "pastry of mockery"—of which many existed and still exist—may be mentioned which to some extent falls outside the majority of gingerbread tentings. These are actually made in two colors. They are baked out of light yellow dough and are triangular in shape, bulging out like a pillow. They are filled with a dark brown mass of similar dough, which seems to well up out of the light dough through a slit in the covering. This package of very ancient usage is euphemistically called a "wind bag," but its correct name is "nun's fart." The interpretation of the name must be more exhaustively treated. "Nun" [*Nonne*] means "lonely, sterile, unfit, injurious"; this is why some destructive insects are designated by this word. This word was already present when women's cloisters came into being, and so their inhabitants were designated by an already available word. The pastry and its name therefore have nothing to do with cloistered women. The modifying word is derived from the root-word "*fas*" and designates offspring. So the whole indicates something begotten by the unfit, something airy or hollow. The giving of such a pastry was an expression of scorn, usually directed toward old maids, or perhaps in another way that mocked some disability. Connected to this are numerous customs practiced on Shrovetide Tuesdays to mock old maids; practices which, however, betray deep meaning. The expression "old furniture" [*altes Möbel*] for older, unmarried girls is not

---

*Therefore fruit kernels and seeds are baked into the three corners, which so well symbolize the three great lights.

in the transferred sense borrowed from an old piece of domestic equipment, but rather directly: "old *moevel* = *meovel* = unfit, infertile. The unmarried status for a girl was, in that era—a time in which marriage was held in high esteem for ecological reasons—no enviable one. Shrovetide Tuesday was the "Shrovetide Thing Day,"[86] a day for holding court, which was originally held in bloody seriousness, and which only later assumed farcical characteristics in Christianized Germania. Numerous customs remind us of this pre-Christian seriousness, among them also the very ancient Viennese folk custom in which the old maids have to rub the tower of Saint Stephen's on Shrovetide Tuesday. This scene forms one element in the program of the different Shrovetide parades every year. This is again *kala* or *heimliche Acht* and is solved according to the code words: "old maids rubbing Stephen's tower" [*alte Jungfer Stephansturm reiben*] as follows: "*mona stafa-thurn ri-ban*," i.e., "unfruitful-steady generation–wend–wax–death or ban"; which means: "from the infertile, who do not live up to their procreative responsibilities, grows death or curses." The contemptuous insult in German: "*das Mensch*" [slut] may have such a curse to thank for its origin. The unfortunate one who escaped death was cursed and forced to do menial tasks of servitude; deprived of her human value, she was now only an object—*das Mensch*.

With these examples about runes, holy signs, symbols, hieroglyphs, etc., neither these themselves nor even the areas in which they occur, have been exhausted—just think of the thousands of pre-Christian sayings. But certainly enough has been shown to indicate that an uncommonly large hoard of such otherwise unperceived mystical signs is present whose meanings are relatively easy to find. But it would have to be the subject and task of a great systematically arranged work to collect all of those signs in their

many interrelations, to refer to all the areas in which
they might be discovered, to ascertain their exact
interpretations, and only on this confirmation to reproduce the old Aryo-Germanic picture writing completely—so that all the scattered pictographic works
can be deciphered with complete certainty to everyone's satisfaction.

This task could not fall to an essay of the kind that
this one represents. It was sufficient here to show and
to confirm by means of incontrovertible proofs (and
we Teutons possess a great hoard of such evidence)
that the seven seals of the secret of the runes and holy
signs have been broken. Emerging from this secret,
however, was a direction of special interest for our
present purposes; and—with the omission of other
disciplines—this study was therefore devoted exclusively to this one direction, i.e., to the old Aryan
worldview as a foundation of the Aryo-Germanic esoteric, and to the ethics and esotericism that results
from this philosophy. The formation of myths, folktales, and sagas, and of customs and practices could
only be considered in passing; the same is true of the
lore of nature, of the earth, and stars, while history
and still other areas of knowledge could receive no
mention at all—for even the main area itself (despite
all efforts at thoroughness and exhaustiveness) could
only be illuminated on the most important points.

The pivotal point of the old Aryo-Germanic worldview laid down in the runes and holy signs and of its
theosophical-metaphysical understanding, however,
rests on the clear understanding of a higher spiritual
being—God!—that[87] consciously and with intention
engendered or created matter, with which it bound
itself indivisibly until their passing away; with matter
equally indivisible from being—ruling within matter—this being controls and develops it until matter
has fulfilled the aim for which it was engendered,
whereupon it will again be dissolved and a higher form

of being—God!—will again be dematerialized as *"Ur,"* which it was before the engendering of the world.

From this main point of understanding, the following points of knowledge may be deduced: (1) the "biune-bifidic dyad" (spirit and body); (2) the "triune-trifidic triad" (Ur–All–Ur, past–present–future, arising–being–passing away to new arising); (3) the "multifidic-multiune multiplicity" (the ego in the All as All); (4) the "divine internity"; since every ego is a part of God, and therefore is immortal as an individual, it consequently only migrates along the way through matter toward eternity through the mutation of uncounted pre-, present-, and post-existences; (5) the "recognition of duty" to help to develop and perfect the work of God; (6) the "will to fulfill this duty," because the will of God must be the personal will of every ego; and (7) the "act of fulfillment," through the sacrifice of one's life.

Upon this esoteric doctrine rest all exoteric teachings; the same appear set down in all attestations of skaldic poetry, as well as in all rules of life and hieroglyphic commandments of the skaldic force of coercion (see p. 101). Just to cite one example: Wuotanism assures those who fall in battle of a heroic heaven with eternal joy in Walhalla. Whoever was killed in battle became one of the *Einherjar*[88]—which excluded renewed existence as a human being—and this was supposed to unite the warrior permanently with the godhead. This is an apparent contradiction of the esoteric teaching—but only an apparent one! The Teuton who trusted in his exoteric faith went to die in battle with firm conviction—with the power of unquestioned autosuggestion!—that he would enter into Walhalla as one of the *Einherjar* (see p. 46ff.), there to enjoy the eternal bliss of battle and love. This unquestioning conviction—whether it arose from knowledge or faith—works as a powerful autosuggestion at the moment of death, and where possible this firm

spiritual conception is promoted by the hypnotic suggestion sent from afar by a skald, a seeress (Albruna),
or by his comrades in arms. This conception (see p.
46 above) was recognized as spiritual protection, which
influenced the conduct of life in the next period of
reincarnation in a determinative way, so that such a
man—as the expression goes—is born already a hero,
in that he begins his next human existence already
more conscious than others, and he has himself born
into appropriate circumstances of life, or when this
does not go smoothly, the unconscious power—the
dark impulse—manifests itself to overcome all re-
stricting limitations in order to reach its goal. Phenomena, such as, for example, a Bismarck, who was
already convinced in his youth that it was his destiny
to unify Germany, are only explicable by means of
such a supposition. On the other hand, the phenomena of personalities such as those who are able to
introduce their trailblazing thoughts to the world only
at an advanced age, without achieving success, are
recognized as spirits who—only beginning to awaken
and to recognize their task too late—are forced to steel
their spiritual power against their—apparent—fail-
ures, in order to complete their unfinished work in
their next rebirth, or perhaps in several renewed human
incarnations. This is possible if they go into death
with the firm conviction of the truth and necessity
of their purpose. In this case, they will present themselves in their next human life as figures such as that
of a Bismarck, a Columbus, a Luther, or many another.* Again, only by means of such a supposition is
it clear why we often have to look back centuries for

*Only from the standpoint of this supposition is a previously
incomprehensible passage in the Bible (Mark 10:29–31) explicable. There Christ speaks directly of rebirth and of the victory of
his idea in a renewed human body: "Many will be the last, who
are the first, and many the first, who are the last."

the origins of ideas that have shaken the world, how they are constantly suppressed and forgotten but again—without perceptible inner context—suddenly flame up again as if born anew to gain final victory. This esoterically explains the exoteric promise of Walhalla, as well as its fulfillment: the *Einherjar* who fall as sacrifices for their ideas, whether on the battlefield, at the stake, or by starvation—the sacrifices of the modern excommunicant, of the boycotted heroes of the spirit—all find in the conviction of their martyrdom that all-conquering bliss and in life after death that state of happiness which determines their next human incarnation and which leads them to a renewed heroic career and to final victory. This is the promised Walhalla: heroic providence in future epochs of life in renewed human bodies.

Those who die a "straw death" [peaceful death in bed] (p. 102) go to "Thrundheim" to become the servants of Thór [Donar]. After what has already been said this needs no further interpretation. Redemption also awaits them in future incarnations, until they are successful in remembering the mission that has become theirs and in fulfilling their task. Thus in the course of uncounted generations all men will become *Einherjar*, and that state—willed and preordained by the godhead—of general liberty, equality, and fraternity will be reached. This is that state which sociologists long for and which socialists want to bring about by false means, for they are not able to comprehend the esoteric concept that lies hidden in the triad: liberty, equality, fraternity, a concept which must first ripen and mature in order that someday it can be picked like a fruit from the World Tree.

That which I have been permitted to offer here in a brief outline as the revealed secret of the runes, appears at first glance to be quite surprising mainly due to its simplicity. However, it may not be overlooked that in spite of this, as one penetrates deeper into the secret, it becomes variously interlaced by all the intertwining and apparently confusing lines in the whirl of which one amazingly comes to understand the "multiune-multifidic multiplicity/unity" of the All—and the godhead itself.

A Short Listian Glossary

All	The objective universe, used by List as a term opposed to the concept of the ego, or *Ich*.
Halgadom	A sanctuary, a "temple site."
heimliche Acht	Probably List's most difficult term to translate, hence it is usually left untranslated. *Heimlich* = "secret," but *Acht* as a noun is used by him in a unique way. The usual translations, either "eight" or "ban; outlawry," are insufficient to account for List's use of the word. With him it is definitely used in the sense of an "underground institution" or "secret tribunal."
kala	From a Sanskrit word, *kalā*, "fractions." Used as a method of calculating the sixteen permutations of the moon, and of determining the esoteric value of syllabic units of sound as they go through similar cyclical permutations.
Rita	From a Sanskrit word, *ṛta*, "cosmic order." List also uses it to mean "sanctified law."
Ur	Used as a prefix in German to indi-

cate the primeval or original quality of something. List uses it as a noun to indicate the undifferentiated primal essence of the universe.

Wihinei   A Listian word for "religion" in its exoteric level as practiced in ancient times.

NOTES

1. Trevor Ravenscroft, *The Spear of Destiny: The Occult Power Behind the Spear Which Pierced the Side of Christ* (New York: G. P. Putnam's Sons, 1973). This is a largely fanciful history which posits that the spear belonging to the Hapsburg Imperial regalia is one and the same with that supposedly used to stab Jesus as he hung on the cross, and that the man who holds this spear holds the destiny of the world in his hands. This book, which was based on ideas given to the author by the Anthroposophist Walter Johannes Stein, also claims that Adolf Hitler was the reincarnation of Landulf II of Padua, who was, it is said, used as a model for Wolfram von Eschenbach's figure of Clinschor (Klingsor) in *Parzival*.

2. Johannes Balzli, *Guido v. List: Der Wiederentdecker uralter Arischer Weisheit—Sein Leben und sein Schaffen* (Vienna: Guido-von-List-Gesellschaft, 1917).

3. Nicholas Goodrick-Clarke, *The Occult Roots of Nazism: The Ariosophists of Austria and Germany, 1890–1935* (Wellingborough, Northamptonshire: Aquarian, 1985). A version of this work was originally presented by the author as a Ph.D. dissertation at Oxford in 1981 with the title *The Ariosophists of Austria and Germany 1890–1935: Reactionary Political Fantasy in Relation to Social Anxiety*.

4. Cf. Balzli, p. 15

5. Guido List, *Deutsch-mythologische Landschaftsbilder* (Berlin: Lüstenöder, 1891), vol. 2, p. 592. The sketches were originally published in Vienna in 1881 in an article entitled "Carnuntum."

6. List, *Deutsch-mythologische Landschaftsbilder*, vol. 2, pp. 592–93.

7. See List, *Deutsch-mythologische Landschaftsbilder*, which is largely made up of reports on such outings. The two most famous of these are the expeditions to the Geiselberg (see note 11, below) and to Carnuntum (see note 6, above).

8. See p. 26ff., below.

9. Balzli, p. 19.

10. See List, *Deutsch-mythologische Landschaftsbilder*, vol. 2, pp. 512–91.

11. This story was published by List several times. It appears in the *Alraunenmären* (Linz: Österreichische Verlagsanstalt, 1903), pp. 397–415, but also in the second edition of the *Deutsch-mythologische Landschaftsbilder* (Vienna: Guido von List Gesellschaft, [1911?]), vol. 1, pp. 117–37, where it is entitled "Auf dem Geiselberg: Eine Weihenacht." There List indicates that it was first published in the *Scheffeljahrbuch* (1893).

12. His political bent is clear from several perspectives, but perhaps the first obvious indications of his political development came in 1877 with his first publication in the Pan-German nationalist newspaper the *Neue Deutsche Alpenzeitung*; see Goodrick-Clarke, pp. 36–38, for an overview of this period in List's life.

13. See p. 27ff. below.

14. For details on the Iduna and its members, see J. W. Nagl and J. Zeidler, *Deutsch-österreichische Literaturgeschichte* (Vienna: Fromme, 1937), vol. 3, pp. 1931–48.

15. See Goodrick-Clarke, p. 39.

16. For a general history of Pan-Germanism, see Andrew G. Whiteside, *Austrian National Socialism before 1918* (The Hague: Nijhoff, 1962), and *The Socialism of Fools* (Berkeley and Los Angeles: University of California Press, 1975). The relationship between this movement and Ariosophy is specifically discussed by Goodrick-Clarke, pp. 7–16.

17. See Carl E. Schorske, *Fin-de-Siècle Vienna* (New York: Vintage, 1981), pp. 120–33 *et passim*, on Schönerer and his influence on contemporary Viennese culture.

18. See Goodrick-Clarke, p. 38.

19. See Balzli, pp. 32–33.

20. The manuscript on *kala* was rejected by the Imperial Academy of Sciences in Vienna (see p. 77ff. of *The Secret of the Runes* for the essentials of this theory); but his theories were eventually fully published in 1914 in his *Ursprache der Ario-Germanen* (see p. 17 below). The article on religious symbols entitled "Die esoterische Bedeutung religiöser Symbole" was published in *Gnosis* (1 [1903], pp. 323–27). It is noteworthy that this was List's first publication in an "occult" journal.

21. For details of this controversy, cf. Goodrick-Clarke, pp. 41–42.

22. See pp. 35–36, below.

23. The pseudonym "Tarnhari" would translate in the Listian linguistic system to "the concealed lord."

24. See Balzli, p. 146; Goodrick-Clarke, pp. 45–46, 84–85.

25. This is the most reliable version (see Goodrick-Clarke, pp. 47–48), but there is also another version that says he died in Vienna on 21 May (see, e.g., Nagl/Zeidler, vol. 3, p. 1935).

26. Guido List, "Götterdämmerung," *Ostdeutsche Rundschau*, 1 Oct. 1893: 1–3.

27. Guido List, "Von der Wuotanspriesterschaft," *Das Zwanzigste Jahrhundert*, 4 (1893): 119–26; 242–51; 343–52; 442–51

28. Guido List, "Die deutsche Mythologie im Rahmen eines Kalenderjahres," *Ostdeutsche Rundschau* (series of eighteen articles which appeared between 14 Jan. and 30 Dec. 1894).

29. Guido List, "Der deutsche Zauberglaube im Bauwesen," *Ostdeutsche Rundschau*, 25 Sept. 1895: 1–2; 26 Sept. 1895: 1–2.

30. Guido List, "Mephistopheles," *Ostdeutsche Rundschau*, 28 Dec. 1895: 1–2; 31 Dec. 1895: 1–3.

31. Historically and archaeologically this would seem to be an inaccurate picture of the situation, as it appears that this territory belonged to the Hallstatt cultural group (proto-Celtic Indo-European) and later to the Celts proper. It was only upon the migrations of the fourth century C. E. that the Germanic cultural wave crossed the Danube from the north, although they may have been in the region to the north of Pannonia much earlier.

32. See Goodrick-Clarke, pp. 62–64, for a brief discussion of these notions. Balzli (p. 55) also gives the same indication of the nature of this work.

33. See, e.g., E. Jung, *Germanische Götter und Helden in christlicher Zeit* (Munich: Lehmann, 1922), pp. 115–26.

34. Ultimately, a study of German and European culture of the nineteenth and early twentieth centuries demonstrates the breadth and depth of the National Socialist brand of racial theory and practice. Efforts to isolate men such as List or Liebenfels as originators of such ideas are simplistic at best; see Peter Viereck, *Metapolitics: The Roots of the Nazi Mind* (New York: Capricorn, 1961).

35. *Kala* is derived from the Sanskrit ferm *kalā*, which is of uncertain etymology. It may be related to *kāla*, "time," yet it is not identical with it. (Note the different vowel length.) The process from which List derived his *kala* is that of determining the "fractions" of the cycle of the moon as it waxes, wanes, disappears, and is reborn. This method of analysis is also applied to the mystical syllables of mantras, etc.; see Mudhu Khanna, *Yantra* (London: Thames and Hudson, 1979), p. 65.

36. This formula is taken from a German translation of an Old Norse verse found in one MS of the "Völuspá" (stanza 64) of the *Poetic Edda*. The phrase in Old Norse, *óflugr ofan* ("the powerful one from above"), and the whole stanza in which it appears are considered by some scholars to be of Christian influence.

37. "Wer ist der Starke von Oben?," *Prana* 7 (1917): 4–5, reprinted in Balzli, pp. 125–33.

38. See, e.g., William E. Coleman, "The Source of Madame Blavatsky's Writings," in Vsevolod S. Soloviev, *A Modern Priestess of Isis* (London: Longmans, Green, 1895), pp. 353–66.

39. The "Aryanization" of Christianity and of the person of Jesus was practiced by Liebenfels, although this idea was broadly represented in *völkisch* circles in the late nineteenth and early twentieth centuries; see Friedrich-Wilhelm Haack, *Wotans Wiederkehr* (Munich: Claudius, 1981), pp. 55–66.

40. This group of writers is identified as having influenced List by Nagl/Zeidler, *Deutsch-österreichische Literaturgeschichte*, vol. 3, p. 1935.

41. For a convenient history of the early investigations of Germanic religion, see Jan de Vries, *Altgermanische Religionsgeschichte* (Berlin: de Gruyter, 1956), vol. 1, p. 50ff.

42. Cf. Walter Kaufmann, *The Portable Nietzsche* (New York: Viking Press, 1954), p. 115ff., and *Nietzsche: Philosopher, Psychologist, Antichrist*, 4th ed. (Princeton: Princeton University Press, 1974), p. 307ff. In the same context, List makes reference to another of Nietzsche's themes—the *ewige Wiederkehr*, "eternal return."

43. It is most probable that List's exposure to Indian religious concepts came through Theosophy; see, e.g., H. P. Blavatsky, *The Secret Doctrine* (Pasadena, Calif.: Theosophical University Press, 1970 [1888]). For a more convenient, scholarly treatment of these concepts, see, e.g., Stephen A. Tyler, *India: An Anthropological Perspective* (Pacific Palisades, Calif.: Goodyear, 1973), pp. 70–71, 98–99.

44. E.g., J. H. Brennan, *The Occult Reich* (New York: Signet, 1974), Gerald Suster, *Hitler: The Occult Messiah* (New York: St. Martin's Press, 1981), and Nigel Pennick, *Hitler's Secret Sciences* (Sudbury, Suffolk: Neville Spearman, 1981).

45. See Goodrick-Clark, pp. 30, 51–52. This influence is fairly clear in the closing pages of the present text.

46. Cf. Goodrick-Clarke, pp. 123–34.

47. The Edda Society, founded by Gorsleben and inherited by von Bülow, officially endorsed National Socialism in 1933 (see Goodrick-Clarke, p. 160), whereas F. B. Marby, especially in his 1935 publications, openly espoused National Socialist ideology; see F. B. Marby, *Rassische Gymnastik als Aufrassungsweg*, Marby-Runen-Bücherei 5/6 (Stuttgart: Marby, 1935), esp. pp. 7–42. His expression of these sentiments is somewhat ironic, since Marby was soon thereafter incarcerated in a concentration camp.

48. A lodge by that name had existed in Scandinavia and Poland from at least the 1600s. However, it had dropped from sight since the late 1700s; see Adolf Hemberger, *Organisationsformen, Rituale, Lehren und magische Thematik der freimauerischen und freimauerartigen Bünde im deutschen Sprachraum Mitteleuropas. Teil I: Der mystisch-magische Orden Fraternitas Saturni* (Frankfurt am Main: Dr. A. Hemberger, 1971), pp. 29, 166.

49. See Hemberger, p. 166.

50. An official branch of the office of Reichsführer SS Heinrich Himmler with the mission of investigating "ancestral heritage"; see Michael H. Kater, *Das "Ahnenerbe" der SS: 1935–1945* (Stuttgart: Deutsche Verlags Anstalt, 1974), and Ulrich Hunger, *Die Runenkunde im Dritten Reich* (Bern: Lang, 1984), pp. 171–289.

51. This was a semiofficial office around Alfred Rosenberg with the unwieldy name and assignment "Dienststelle des Beauftragten des Führers für die gesamte geistige und weltanschauliche Schulung und Erziehung des NSDAP"; see Hunger, pp. 108–132.

52. A complete study of Wiligut was done by the former ONT brother and Waffen-SS officer Rudolf J. Mund, *Der Rasputin Himmlers: Die Wiligut Saga* (Vienna: Volkstum-Verlag, 1982), see also Goodrich-Clarke, pp. 177–91 and Hunger, pp. 164–66.

53. See Hunger, pp. 161–62.

54. She was the wife of the treasurer of the Edda Society (Freidrich Schaefer), and she provided a meeting point for different rune-occultist circles—including that of Karl Maria Wiligut; see Goodrick-Clarke, pp. 159, 183.

55. See note 42, above.

56. Cf. "Hávamál," stanza 139. The Old Norse reads: *gefinn Ódhni, sjálfr sjálfum mér,* "given to Ódhinn, myself to myself."

57. The German prefix *ur-*, which indicates the original or primal state of something, is here used as a noun. This will sometimes be left as "the *Ur*," while at other times it will be translated as "primal," "primeval," or some other appropriate term.

58. See the discussion of the "gibor-rune" on pp. 65–67, below.

59. Cf. Mark 11:23.

60. This is related to the *ægis-hjálmer*, the helm of awe or terror, which was a part of the Nibelungen treasure won by Sigurdhr.

61. Here we see the origins of the chant used by the Germanen Orden, which later became a National Socialist motto: *Sieg Heil!*, 'Hail Victory!'

62. Cf. note 64, below.

63. From "Hávamál," stanza 84.

64. In German *der Mensch* means "human, man," whereas *das Mensch* means "slut, ruined woman."

65. Here List includes the sacral kings of Egypt among the Aryans.

66. List: *Truthenfuss*, standard modern German: *Drudenfuss*, the foot of a *Drude*; pentagram. *Drude:* "a dangerous female numen of the night," cf. Old Norse *Thrudhr*, old English *dhrydh*: "a wood maiden." Cf. further Jacob Grimm, *Teutonic Mythology*, vol. 1, pp. 422–23.

67. In this formula, *Saal*, List has conflated three German words and concepts, (1) *Saal*, "hall" (derived from Proto-Germanic *salaz, "hall, temple"), (2) *sal*, "pale, feeble," cf. English "sallow"), and (3) *Sal*, "legal transfer of property" (an old legal term, cf. English "sale").

68. *Schöffe* or *Schöppe* was an archaic Vehmic title for the magistrate or juryman. List is using a play on the German words *Schöpfer*, "creator (shaper)," and *Schöpfer*, "ladle (scooper)."

69. The two German words used here are related to the word for "hat," *der Hut*, i.e., *die Hut*, "shelter," and *die Hütung*, "the guarding."

70. *Minne* is an archaic Germanic word for love of a spiritual or "ideal" type. It is contrasted with *Liebe*, love of a physical kind. Linguistically, *Minne* is related to the concept of "memory."

71. In modern German *sittlich* means "moral, ethical, or customary."

72. "Song of the Nibelungs," anonymous thirteenth-century German version of the *Völsung* material.

73. "Poor Heinrich," a thirteenth-century German epic by Hartmann von Aue.

74. There is a wordplay here with the German words for "body" (*Leib*) and for "loaf" (*Laib*).

75. Typically, small German loaves of bread, as for instance the "Kaiser" roll, have a depression of some kind in the center.

76. The name of the roll, *Wecken*, is related to the word "wedge," and not to the German word for "awaken," *wecken*.

77. The *Kipfel* bread-shape is named after the upright staves on the sides of a wagon. Ultimately it is derived from the Latin *cippus*, "stake."

78. The "wending horn" is a name given to the shape thought to be a combination of the man-rune ᛉ and the yr-rune ᛦ , life and death respectively. It is considered to be a sign of the "tree of life."

79. A roll. Ultimately derived from Latin *simila*, "the finest wheat flour," which in turn was derived through Greek from the Semitic (Akkadian) *samīdu*, "fine wheat flour."

80. Here List puns on the words *mahlen* "to mill, grind," and *ver-mählen*, "to marry." Actually, while *vermählen* comes from the Old High German *mahal*, "the place of the legal assembly"—where marriage contracts were made—*mahlen* or *mählen* is derived from a root meaning "to grind."

81. The word appears actually to be derived from Latin *brachitum*, "bread in the shape of crossed arms."

82. From Old High German *krapfo*, "hook, bent claw." A form of fried pastry much like a jelly-filled doughnut.

83. "Fasching" is Karneval, Shrovetide, or the pre-Lenten festival, the particulars of which certainly originated in pagan practice. The word *Fasching* is derived from Middle High German *vastschang*, "the pouring out of drink on the eve of fasting."

84. The word is derived from Old High German *flado*, a type of sacrificial cake. Its name ultimately refers to its broad and flat shape.

85. The *Stritzel* means the "straw maid" and the "straw widower" (or "widow").

86. Here List correctly makes the connection between *Dienstag* [Tuesday] and the Germanic institution of the *thing*, "legal assembly." *Dienstag = Dings-tag*, "thing's day." By contrast, the English name *Tues-day* is derived from the name of the Germanic god of law and justice, Tiw. The German names the institution, while the English names the god who presides over it.

87. Here List uses the neuter relative pronoun, which indicates either that the antecedent is "being," i.e., "essence" and not the masculine "God," or that he has reverted to the ancient gender of "God" as being neuter.

88. An Old Norse term, singular: *einheri*, "a single combatant," the title of those human warriors whom the *valkyrjur* (Valkyries) have chosen to populate the heavenly army of Wuotan—in anticipation of the final cosmic battle *ragnarök*, "the fate of the gods."

BIBLIOGRAPHY

Balzli, Johannes. *Guido v. List: Der Wiederentdecker urlater Arischer Weisheit—Sein Leben und sein Schaffen.* Vienna: Guido-von-List-Gesellschaft, 1917.

Blavatsky, H. P. *The Secret Doctrine.* 2 vols. Pasadena, Calif.: Theosophical University Press, 1970 [1888].

Brennan, J. H. *The Occult Reich.* New York: Signet, 1974.

Colman, William E. "The Source of Madame Blavatsky's Writings." In *A Modern Priestess of Isis,* edited by Vsevolod Soloviev. London: Longmans, Green, 1895.

Goodrick-Clarke, Nicholas. *The Occult Roots of Nazism: The Ariosophists of Austria and Germany, 1890–1935.* Wellingborough, Northamptonshire: Aquarian, 1985.

Grimm, Jacob. *Teutonic Mythology.* 4 vols. New York: Dover, 1966 [1835, first German ed.].

Haack, Friedrich-Wilhem. *Wotans Wiederkehr.* Munich: Claudius, 1981.

Hemberger, Adolf. *Organisationsformen, Rituale, Lehren und magische Thematik der freimauerischen und freimauer artigen Bunde im deutschen Sprachraum Mitteleuropas. Teil I. Der mystisch-magische Orden Fraternitas Saturni.* Frankfurt am Main: Dr. A. Hemberger, [1971].

Hollander, Lee M. *The Poetic Edda.* Austin: University of Texas Press, 1962.

Hunger, Ulrich. *Die Runenkunde im Dritten Reich.* Bern: Lang, 1984.

Jossé, Roland Dionys. *Die Tala der Raunen (Runo-astrologische Kabbalistik).* Freiburg im Breisgau: Bauer, 1955.

Jung, E. *Germanische Götter und Helden in christlicher Zeit.* Munich: Lehmann, 1922.

Kater, Michael H. *Das "Ahnenerbe" der SS: 1935–1945.* Stuttgart: Deutsche Verlags Anstalt, 1974.

Kaufmann, Walter. *The Portable Nietzsche.* New York: Viking Press, 1954.

———. *Nietzsche: Philosopher, Psychologist, Antichrist.* 4th ed. Princeton: Princeton University Press, 1974.

Khanna, Mudhu. *Yantra.* London: Thames and Hudson, 1979.

Kosbab, Werner. *Das Runen-Orakel.* Freiburg im Breisgau: Bauer, 1981.

Kummer, Siegfried Adolf. *Heilige Runenmacht: Wiedergeburt des Armanentums durch Runenübungen und Tänze.* Hamburg: Uranus, 1932.

———. *Runen-Magie.* (= Germanische Schriftenfolge 4) Dresden: K. Hartmann, 1933.

List, Guido (von). *Carnuntum.* Berlin: Grot'sche Verlags-buchhandlung, 1888.

———. *Deutsch-mythologische Landschaftsbilder.* 2 vols. Berlin: H. Lüstenöder, 1891.

———. "Von der Wuotanspriesterschaft." *Das Zwanzigste Jahrhundert* 4 (1893): 119–26; 242–51; 343–52; 442–51.

———. "Gotterdämmerung." *Ostdeutsche Rundschau,* 1 Oct. 1893, pp. 1–3.

———. *Jung Diethers Heimkehr.* Brünn: "Deutsches Haus," 1894.

———. "Der deutsche Zauberglaube im Bauwesen." *Ostdeutsche Rundschau,* 25 Sept. 1895, pp. 1–2; 26 Sept. 1985, pp. 1–2.

———. "Mephistopheles." *Ostdeutsche Rundschau,* 28 Dec. 1895, pp. 1–2; 31 Dec. 1895, pp. 1–3.

———. *Pipara: die Germanin im Cäsarenpurpur.* Leipzig: A. Schulze, 1895.

———. *Walkürenweihe.* Brünn: "Deutsches Haus," 1895.

———. *Der Unbesiegbare: Ein Grundzug germanischer Weltanschauung.* Vienna: C. Vetter, 1898.

———. *König Vannius.* Brünn: "Deutsches Haus," 1899.

———. *Der Wiederaufbau von Carnuntum.* Vienna: F. Schalk, 1900.

———. *Sommer-Sonnwend-Feuerzauber. Skaldisches Weihespiel.* Vienna: F. Schalk, 1901.

———. *Alraunenmären.* Linz: Österreichische Verlagsanstalt, 1903.

———. "Die esoterische Bedeutung religiöser Symbole." *Gnosis* 1 (1903): 323–27.

———. *Das Goldstück: Ein Liebesdrama in fünf Aufzügen.* Vienna: Literatur-Anstalt Austria, 1903.

――. *Das Geheimnis der Runen.* Guido-von-List-Bücherei (hereafter GvLB) 1. Gross-Lichterfelde: P. Zillmann, [1907/08].

――. *Die Armanenschaft der Ario-Germanen I.* GvLB 2a. Vienna: Guido-von-List-Gesellschaft, 1908.

――. *Die Rita der Ario-Germanen.* GvLB 3. Vienna: Guido-von-List-Gesellschaft, 1908.

――. *Die Namen der Völkerstämme Germaniens und deren Deutung.* GvLB 4. Vienna: Guido-von-List-Gesellschaft, 1909.

――. *Die Bilderschrift der Ario-Germanen: Ario-Germanische Hieroglyphik.* GvLB 5. Vienna: Guido-von-List-Gesellschaft, 1910.

――. *Die Religion der Ario-Germanen in ihrer Esoterik und Exoterik.* Leipzig: Bürdeke, [1910].

――. *Die Armanenschaft der Ario-Germanen II.* GvLB 2b. Vienna: Guido-von-List-Gesellschaft, 1911.

――. *Deutsch-mythologische Landschaftsbilder.* 2nd ed. Vienna: Guido-von-List-Gesellschaft, [1911].

――. *Die Urspraches der Ario-Germanen und ihre Mysteriensprache.* GvLB 6. Vienna: Guido-von-List-Gesellschaft, 1914.

――. "Wer ist der Starke von Oben?" *Prana* 7 (1917). Reprinted in Balzli, pp. 125–33.

――. *Der Übergang vom Wuotanismus zum Christentum.* Berlin-Lichterfelde: G. v. List, 1926 [orig. 1911].

Marby, Friedrich Bernhard. *Runenschrift, Runenwort, Runengymnastik.* Marby-Runen-Bücherei 1/2. Stuttgart: Marby, 1931.

――. *Marby-Runen-Gymnastik.* Marby-Runen-Bücherei 3/4. Stuttgart: Marby, 1932.

――. *Rassische Gymnastik als Aufrassungsweg.* Marby-Runen-Bücherei 5/6. Stuttgart: Marby, 1935.

――. *Die Rosengarten und das ewige Land der Rasse.* Marby-Runen-Bücherei 7/8. Stuttgart: Marby, 1935.

Mone, Friedrich Josef. *Geschichte des Heidentums im nördlichen Europa.* 2 vols. Darmstadt: Leste, 1921–24.

Mund, Rudolf J. *Der Rasputin Himmlers: Die Wiligut Saga.* Vienna: Volkstum-Verlag, 1982.

Nagl, J. W., and J. Zeidler. *Deutsch-österreichische Literaturgeschichte.* 3 vols. Vienna: Fromme, 1937.

Pennick, Nigel. *Hitler's Secret Sciences.* Sudbury, Suffolk: Neville Spearman, 1981.

Ravenscroft, Trevor. *The Spear of Destiny: The Occult Power Behind the Spear Which Pierced the Side of Christ.* New York: G. P. Putnam's Sons, 1973.

Reynitzsch, Wilhelm. *Über Truhten and Trutensteine, Barden und Bardenlieder, Feste, Schmäuse, usw. und Gerichte der Teutschen*. Gotha: Ettinger, 1802.

Schorske, Carl E. *Fin-de-Siècle Vienna*. New York: Vintage, 1981.

Simrock, Karl. *Die Edda*. Stuttgart: Cotta, 1851.

———. *Handbuch der deutschen Mythologie mit Einschluss der nordischen*. Bonn: Marcus, 1853.

Spiesberger, Karl. *Runenmagie*. Berlin: Schikowski, 1955.

Suster, Gerald. *Hitler: The Occult Messiah*. New York: St. Martin's Press, 1981.

Tacitus, Cornelius. *The Agricola and the Germania*. Translated by H. Mattingly. Harmondsworth, UK: Penguin, 1970.

Thorsson, Edred. *Futhark: A Handbook of Rune Magic*. York Beach, Maine: Samuel Weiser, 1984.

Tyler, Stephen A. *India: An Anthropological Perspective*. Pacific Palisades, Calif.: Goodyear, 1973.

Uhland, Ludwig. *Sagenforschungen*. Hildesheim: Olms, 1972 [1868].

Viereck, Peter. *Metapolitics: The Roots of the Nazi Mind*. New York: Capricorn, 1961.

Vollmer, Wilhelm. *Vollständiges Wörterbuch der Mythologie aller Nationen*. Stuttgart: Hoffmann, 1836.

Vries, Jan de. *Altgermanische Religionsgeschichte*. 2 vols. Berlin: de Gruyter, 1956–57.

Whiteside, Andrew G. *Austrian National Socialism before 1918*. The Hague: Nijhoff, 1962.

———. *The Socialism of Fools: Georg Ritter von Schönerer and Austrian Pan-Germanism*. Berkeley and Los Angeles: University of California Press, 1975.

Wiligut, Karl Maria, *Seyfrids Runen*. Vienna: F. Schalk, 1903.

INDEX